'BEING'

the teaching of Advaita

A Basic Introductrion

Philip Jacobs

THE STUDY SOCIETY

Also by Philip Jacobs:

One Self, Life as a Means of Transformation, pub. O Books, 2006

Other Study Society publications:

Birth and Death
The Bridge
Fresh Mornings of Life
Good Company ISBN 0-9547939-0-0
A Lasting Freedom
The Man Who Wanted to Meet God ISBN 0-517-88520-4
The Orange Book ISBN 0-9547939-3-5
Prayer
Voyage of Discovery ISBN 0-9547939-4-3
Who Am I? ISBN 0-9547939-2-7

‘BEING’

the teaching of Advaita

A Basic Introductrion

ISBN 0 - 9547939 - 6 - X

A catalogue record for this book is available
from the British Library

Published in 2007 by The Society for the Study
of Normal Psychology, Colet House, 151 Talgarth Road, London W14 9DA
Telephone 00 44 (0) 208 748 9338,
Fax: 00 44 (0) 208 563 0551
Email: colethouse@clara.net
Website: http://www.studysociety.net

The Study Society has groups around the UK, and can also be contacted
through addresses in Australia, Mexico, New York and New Zealand

Printed in Great Britain by
Creative Print and Design (Wales), Ebbw Vale

CONTENTS

ACKNOWLEDGEMENTS

The Study Society would like to thank the following individuals, organisations and publishers for kindly granting permission to use copyright material:

The Reverend Keith Ward for permission to quote from his talk given at Colet House.

Lucia Van der Post for permission to quote the words of her father, Sir Laurens Van der Post.

Fair Winds Press for permission to quote Christopher Titmus in "The Awakening West".

Shambhala Publications Inc. for permission to quote from "One Taste", "The Eye of Spirit" and "A Brief History of Everything" by Ken Wilber.

The Zen Trust for permission to quote from "The Ceasing of Notions".

Beacon Press for permission to quote from "Man's Search for Meaning" by Viktor Frankl.

Sri Ramanasramam for permission to quote Sri Ramana Maharshi from "Self Enquiry", "Who Am I?", "Maharshi's Gospel", "Talks with Ramana Maharshi" and "Letters from Sri Ramanasramam".

HarperCollins publishers for permission to reprint 30 words from "The Light Around the Body" by Robert Bly.

HarperCollins publishers for permission to quote P.J. Kavanagh in "The Case Against God" by Gerald Priestland.

Oxford University Press for permission to quote from "The Acts of Thomas" in the "Apocryphal New Testament".

Coleman Barks for permission to quote his Rumi translations in "One Handed Basket Weaving".

John Wolters for permission to quote from "Revelations of Divine Love" by Julian of Norwich.

E.J. Brill for permission to quote from "The Gospel of Thomas" from "The Nag Hammadi Library".

New World Library, CA for permission to reprint from the book "The Power of Now", copyright 1999 by Eckhart Tolle.

The Random House Group for permission to reprint from "The Way of the White Clouds" by Lama Anagarika Govinda, published by Rider.

The Random House Group for permission to reprint from "Glimpse after Glimpse" by Sogyol Rinpoche, published by Rider.

Random House Inc. for permission to quote from the Doubleday edition of "Healing into Life and Death" by Stephen Levine.

New Directions Publishing for permission to quote from "Siddhartha" by Herman Hesse.

The Trustees of the E.J.W. Gibb Memorial Trust for permission to quote from the "Mathnawi of Jalaluddin Rumi" translated by Dr Reynold Nicholson.

Dr Wendy Roles for permission to quote the words of Dr Francis Roles.

A.P. Watt on behalf of Michael B. Yeats for permission to quote from "The Winding Stair" by W.B. Yeats.

I would also like to thank Solveig McIntosh for her help in the preparation of the text.

BIBLIOGRAPHY

Anderson, William (1988), *Cecil Collins, The Quest for the Great Happiness*, Barrie and Jenkins.

Blofield, John (1968), *The Zen Teaching of Huang Po*, The Buddhist Society.

Bly, Robert (1967), *The Light Around the Body*, Harper Collins.

Campbell, Joseph (1988), *The Power of Myth*, Doubleday.

Carlson, Richard and Shield, Benjamin, eds. (1996), *Handbook for the Soul*, Piatkus.

Dethlefsen, Thorwald and Dahlke, Rudiger (1990), *The Healing Power of Illness*, Element.

Dumitriu, Petru, *Incognito*, Collins

Evans-Wentz, ed. (1954), *The Tibetan Book of the Great Liberation*, Oxford University Press.

Fenwick, Peter (1995), *The Truth in the Light*, Hodder Headline.

Fox, Matthew (1983), *Original Blessing*, Bear & Co.

Frankl, Viktor (1984), *Man's Search for Meaning*, Beacon Press

Govinda, Anagarika (1992), *The Way of the White Clouds*, Rider.

Hesse, Herman, *Siddhartha*, New Directions Publishing.

Hoff, Benjamin (1989), *The Tao of Pooh*, Mandarin.

Jacobs, Philip (2006), *One Self*, O Books.

James, M.R. trans, (1924), Acts of Thomas from the *Apocryphal New Testament*, Oxford University Press.

Julian of Norwich (1966), *Revelations of Divine Love*, Penguin.

Levine, Stephen (1987), *Healing into Life and Death*, Anchor Books.

Levine, Stephen (1984), *Meetings at the Edge*, Gateway Books.

Lao Tzu (1988), trans; Stephen Mitchell, *Tao te Ching*, Harper Collins.

Lumiere, Lynn Marie and Lumiere-Wins, John (2003), *The Awakening West*, Fair Winds Press.

Moore, Thomas (1992), *Care of the Soul*, Harper Collins.

Nag Hammadi Library (1977), *Gospel of Thomas*, E.J. Brill, Leiden.

Ouspensky, P.D. (1981), *Tertium Organum*, Routledge and Kegan Paul.

Ouspensky, P.D. (1938), *A New Model of the Universe*, Routledge and Kegan Paul.

Priestland, Gerald (1984), *The Case Against God,* Collins.

Ramana Maharshi (1971), *Self Enquiry*, Sri Ramanasramam.

Ramana Maharshi (1969), *Who Am I?*, Sri Ramanasramam.

Ramana Maharshi, *Maharshi's Gospel*, Sri Ramanasramam.

Ramana Maharshi, *Talks with Ramana Maharshi*, Sri Ramanasramam.

Ramana Maharshi, *Letters from Sri Ramanasramam*, Sri Ramanasramam.

Ritchie, George (1978), *Return from Tomorrow*, Kingsway.

Roles, Francis, *Waking Up*, The Study Society, London

Roles, Francis (1972), *A Lasting Freedom*, The Study Society, London.

Roles, Francis (1977), *The Unity of Conscious Experience,* The Society for the Study of Human Being, Inc.

Roles, Francis (1992), *Voyage of Discovery*, The Society for the Study of Human Being, Inc.

Rumi, Jalaluddin, trans. Reynold Nicholson (1925), *The Mathnawi*, Luzac & Co.

Rumi, Jalaluddin, trans. Coleman Barks (1991), *One Handed Basket Weaving*, Maypop.

Saraswati, Shantananda (1981), *A Method of Self Realisation, (The Orange Book)*, Wellington Study Group, Inc.

Saraswati, Shantananda (1987), *Good Company*, The Study Society, London.

Saraswati, Shantananda (1996), *The Man Who Wanted to Meet God*, Bell Tower.

Shankara, trans. Swami Madhavananda (1944), *Viveka-Chudamani*, Advaita Ashrama.

Soko, Morinaga Roshi (1988), *The Ceasing of Notions*, The Zen Centre.

Sibley, Brian, *Shadowlands*, Hodder and Stoughton.

Thomas, Helen, *World Without End*, Faber and Faber.

Watts, Alan (1936), *The Spirit of Zen*, John Murray.

Wilber, Ken (2000), *One Taste*, Shambhala.

Wilber, Ken (1998), *The Eye of Spirit*, Shambhala.

Wilber, Ken (1996), *A Brief History of Everything*, Shambhala.

Yeats, W.B. (1974), *Selected Poetry*, Pan Books Ltd.

INTRODUCTION

Dr Roles, towards the end of his life, said that he thought we needed a simple basic introductory course in the non-dual teaching for newer people. I was also aware that during his last year he was, through his own experience, developing a different approach so that at times he appeared frustrated at our inability to grasp what he was saying. He summed up this approach during his last Sunday meeting as follows:

> "The need now is for simplicity. We have been habitually complicating everything. It is only necessary to be quiet and to keep things simple. We have had everything upside down and back to front.
>
> There is only one Consciousness. The levels are levels of impediment to that Consciousness. Everything is that Consciousness. That is what we have to feel and know."

However, that was said quite a few years ago and, as the Benedictine monk Bede Griffiths once pointed out, any revelation is limited by its manifestation in time and space. While we may continue to make references to past sources, it is important that the teaching is continually reformulated by each new generation in a way that is appropriate for the times, that it is based on deep inner experience and that it is the outflowing from the One Source in the present.

What seemed to be a new approach for Dr Roles has now, I feel, "come of age" and is widely available. This framework is an attempt both to carry out Dr Roles' wishes for an introductory course and to develop and expand his final direction in a way that is relevant for today.

All the various concepts in Advaita are metaphorical ways of expressing the one fundamental truth, and different people find different approaches helpful. Some want a lot of information and detail while others just want the basic framework that can be carried around during the day. Whatever our individual preference, the important thing is not to lose sight of the essential truth of the Unity and Oneness of all Creation and the illusion of our separation.

Ultimately Reality can never be expressed in words so it is for each individual to see beyond the different metaphors and make their own formulation from direct experience.

Philip Jacobs

Part One

THE WAY OF UNDERSTANDING AND THE JOURNEY OF LIFE

The story of The Study Society

The work of the Study Society centred on Colet House was started by the Russian philosopher, writer and mathematician P.D. Ouspensky. He was convinced that there existed a system of thought that lay behind the various religious and philosophical systems and schools of yoga. During the last century he had travelled extensively looking for traces of this system. But with the outbreak of the First World War his search in India was interrupted. Although during the rest of his life he found many ideas and methods that he believed had originated from this source, he was unable to make contact with the tradition itself.

Ouspensky's successor was a man named Dr Francis Roles. Before his death in 1947 Ouspensky asked Dr Roles to continue his search to find this tradition and a simple method to enable man to realise his full potential, that he believed existed with it.

It was not until 1961, when Dr Roles met Shantananda Saraswati, the Shankaracharya of Northern India, head of the Non Dualistic or Advaita tradition with its simple system of knowledge and meditation, that he realised that he had fulfilled Ouspensky's wishes. All quotations in the text acknowledged as 'The Shankaracharya' refer to this Teacher. For this tradition, although existing in the Indian culture, has always been an advisory tradition for people of all faiths, beliefs and backgrounds.

During the following twenty years Dr Roles and some of his colleagues made regular visits to India for audiences with the Shankaracharya, and it is the record of these audiences that form the basis of our study at Colet House.

Also in 1963 the Society made contact with another of the world's great Non Dualistic traditions, the Mevlevi Order of

Dervishes, founded by the 13th century Persian poet and mystic, Jalaluddin Rumi. One of the sheikhs, Resuhi Baykara, came to London to teach the turning ceremony, and it has been practised and taught at Colet on a regular basis ever since.

Before his death in 1982 Dr Roles expressed the wish that the Study Society of the future should be "a cell of Self knowledge", a place that people could come to for "rest and refreshment", "particularly the young for whom life is very difficult today." He said that we should be "a body of people who provide help", and that Colet is a place where the Non Dualistic teaching, the meditation, the turning and other sacred dances and methods are available for those who want them.

The Way of Understanding

This particular path we study is often known as the 'Way of the Householder', since it is suitable for people living busy lives, earning their living and raising families, as opposed to some full time arduous ways that may require that one retires from the world and lives in a monastery.

It is also known as 'The Way of Understanding'. It is called this because no discipline is imposed from outside, but rather it is up to each individual to find what is suitable for them and what works for them. For example, no one tells you that you have to meditate, but if you do it and you find it makes your life brighter, then you naturally want to do more.

So our own individual lives become our paths to the realisation of our true Selves. Rumi, writing in his epic poem, 'The Mathnawi', tells the story of a man who lived in Baghdad and dreamt that there was a great treasure in a particular house in Cairo. After many adventures and trials he arrived at the house in Cairo and all he found there was a man who said that he had dreamt that there was a great treasure in a particular house in Baghdad, which the first man recognised as his own house. So he returned home and sure enough found the treasure.

This story illustrates the fact that we already are that which we are seeking, yet paradoxically it is often the journey of life that brings us to this realisation. Then all the different aspects of life become necessary parts of this journey; both the developing of our talents and the things we love, and also the more difficult aspects of life such as illness and loss. It is as if we are being led through a set course of experience to learn certain things, especially about the process of shedding lesser levels of identity and discovering who we really are.

In this way the teaching is usually discussed and assimilated in groups. There are two particular reasons for this. Firstly, because working on one's own it is easy to become disheartened, and so it's very helpful to have encouragement from other like-minded people. And secondly, no individual knows it all, so in a group you get a much fuller picture as each member is able to include their own very valid experience and understanding.

Quotations

"I've always felt that life is an immense journey, where you leave, as it were, what made you, leave everything you are, and you go on a journey, and in a tremendous round about way, you come back to it, to rediscover it, to be reunited with it in a much greater, more meaningful way, than you could have been if you had not been separated and exiled from it."
Sir Laurens van der Post

"There is something in each person which is better than it is in anybody else. We have to be true to this, and we have to go for Self-realisation from this, so we have to know ourselves. Each person has a strength or a skill or a beauty – something which has no equal anywhere else – and from this we'll succeed in Self-realisation." *Dr Roles*

"We can do something useful in line with the Param Atman. There's never a moment when we cannot do something; but this discipline must come from inside. It cannot be imposed by an external organisation, and it comes through love. When realised that we have nothing of our own, all doors open to us." *Dr Roles*

"There is something or other in all of use which is special or outstanding. For example: some are intelligent, some

are unintelligent, some are strong and some are weak; some are learned and some are ignorant; some are rich and some are poor.

Each should try to please God (or serve God, or worship God, as the case may be) with that attribute chiefly in which he excels. This is the path of least resistance. It is sure to work, as it has always done in the past."

The Shankaracharya

"When the journey back home starts, this discrimination has to be done by the disciple himself – to discriminate what comes from the causal body and what are outer influences – he does not have to stop and enquire but go direct to the Absolute or Atman.

Once, through meditation, one gets the taste of inner happiness which is not available in the physical world, then one wants to have it again and again. In the same way, you can drop a few grains of sugar but you do not have to create a road for the ant to travel from one grain to another. Once it has tasted the sugar, the ant will find its way to the next grain. It is the same for oneself. One gets the taste of inner happiness one does not need anyone's help because one is capable of taking the journey oneself."

The Shankaracharya

"A simple reversal of thinking is necessary, e.g. we think we are being carried inexorably toward our death, but in reality we are being lovingly carried toward our birth. That's why we can have confidence, and let the old drop off like old clothes, old suffering, old sins that we are attached to. Let us do what we do well, learn to use our gifts, develop what we love. Have confidence." *Dr Roles*

"Some people wrongly believe Karma means that if we have done bad things in the past, bad things happen to us in the present. This is just fear mongering. Karma is the most merciful process. It teaches us – subtly, gently, lovingly – what we need to know, and keeps amplifying it until we can

hear it. What could be more exquisite than a teacher able to help us remove the obstructions to the natural brilliancy of the soul?[25]" Stephen Levine

"'Do you ever have this sense when you are following your bliss, as I have at moments, of being helped by hidden hands?'

'All the time. It is miraculous. I even have a superstition that has grown on me as a result of invisible hands coming all the time – namely, that if you do follow your bliss you put yourself on a kind of track that has been there all the while, waiting for you, and the life that you ought to be living is the one you are living. When you can see that, you begin to meet people who are in the field of your bliss, and they open the doors to you. I say, follow your bliss and don't be afraid, and doors will open where you didn't know they were going to be.'"[1] Joseph Campbell

Part Two

NON-DUALITY AND THE FOUR LEVELS

Non-duality is a universal teaching that is not the exclusive property of any particular tradition, but is to be found as the basis of all the world's great religious and mystical traditions. But there is one difficulty in coming to understand it which is that it is a model of experience and so cannot be explained rationally. It is purely a matter of direct experience which can be hinted at by metaphors and symbols. Thus it can appear paradoxical, not because it is, but because this is how reality appears when viewed from a purely rational perspective.

Non-duality literally means 'not two' and implies that the whole universe and everything in it is all the manifestation of One Universal Consciousness, and yet we mistakenly see the world and ourselves as separate realities. It is as if there is just One Consciousness looking out through all of our different eyes.

In the Advaita tradition two Sanskrit words are used to express this Consciousness, "Param Atman" which literally means "Great Spirit" and "Atman" which means "Spirit" and refers to that aspect of the Universal Consciousness in each individual. Although two words are used for the purposes of training, as we shall see there is in reality no difference between the two.

The Four Levels

One of the ways of approaching the concept of non-duality is through the teaching of the four levels. The idea of Consciousness manifesting in Creation through a series of levels like a spectrum is also common to many of the great religious traditions. In the early Christian church there existed the concept of body, soul and spirit. This is a very useful model. If you just have a body and soul it implies that God is somewhere outside, external and separate. With a body, soul and spirit, God is no longer external but is one with our deepest identity.

In the Advaita tradition Consciousness is described as manifesting through four levels: physical, subtle, causal and Divine.

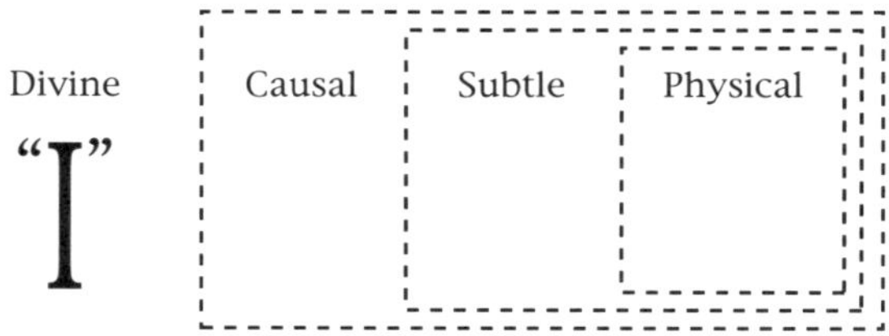

The physical level on the individual scale is our physical body that we can see and touch. It is composed of flesh and bones, internal organs and neuro-chemical mechanisms. It can be weighed, measured and observed by science. It is subject to time and space, birth and death, growth and decay.

The subtle level is the realm of our individual psyches. It is here that we experience our thoughts, feelings and desires. As it cannot be observed by other people its content is known only to the individual through direct experience. Aspects of it will naturally be reflected on the physical level through our body language, in the way that our expressions and postures spontaneously portray such emotions as happiness or sadness, rigidity or openness, anger or fear.

The causal level is described as having two aspects. On one level it is like an unmanifest storehouse of talents, memories, knowledge and impressions, like an enfolded blue print or film. Part of this level is built up through the repetition of experience during childhood and later life. Habitual modes of behaviour eventually become a "part of our nature" at this level. It is rather like a coloured slide in a projector through which the light of Consciousness shines, giving rise to all the individuality and local colour in our characters. The whole of an individual's life path is enfolded at this level. Sometimes we get intimations of it as if there is a vague memory of what is to come or of what we have to do.

The other aspect of the causal body or causal level is sometimes described as a formless realm or unmanifest potential. It is like a great emptiness that is also a great fullness. It is total stillness and immobility. When we look for the source of our thoughts or the source of our dreams or the source of our sense of 'I' all we find is this vast 'emptiness' at the centre of our Being. It is from this realm of 'emptiness' that everything is unfolding and returning. It is a realm of no experience, all experience, happens through the subtle and physical body. It is sometimes described as being like a mirror or pond in which the light of pure Consciousness is reflected.

The Divine body is the ground of all Being. It is the pure Consciousness that underlies all the manifest physical and psychological forms and through which it manifests. This is our true nature and at this level there ceases to be any separation between individuals and the whole manifest creation. This is not a remote far away idealised level which is only obtainable after years of struggle. Nor are the levels or bodies separate. Each level is enfolded in the one above and is just a partial understanding of it. It is not a question of levels of Consciousness for there is nowhere that Consciousness is more or less present. It is present equally everywhere. It is more a question of levels of mistaken identity.

The concept of four levels can also be applied to the world around: the physical world is the whole of the manifest universe, ranging from atomic particles through to planets, solar systems, galactic clusters to the universe of two hundred billion galaxies. At one level it can all be observed by science. When we look up at the stars stretching across a clear night sky we realise that the immensity we see is just an atom of the totality. All this is contained in and is an expression of a universal subtle world, a universal world of mind and memory. This too is an expression of the causal world. It is like a universal blueprint in which the laws of nature are enfolded, existing in potential. This again is all an expression of One Universal Consciousness. From the point of view of this model, Consciousness is not a remote principle lying behind the universe. The whole manifest creation is an expression of this great stillness. It is not that Consciousness is in matter but that matter is in Consciousness and is but a ripple on the surface of this vastness.

Quotations

"There is only one Consciousness. The levels are levels of impediment to that Consciousness. Everything is that Consciousness. That is what we have to feel and know."

Dr Roles

"Although individuals do feel a separate identity, in reality there is only one identity, and that is the Param Atman."

The Shankaracharya

"Within and without are the same. The Absolute is in all. All beings are a part of the same. Everything exists in Atman and it is also reflected in the human form. Wherever you look, you look at the Atman. It is not so much a question of looking within or without, but a question of looking rightly or wrongly." *The Shankaracharya.*

"If a coiled piece of rope is lying where there is not enough light, one may think it is a snake. Then with the thought that it is a snake there comes a fear of death, but that can be removed by a flood of light – this knowledge that it is not a snake.

When by the light of discrimination one understands that this is not real, and that it is all a manifestation of God himself – the Lord Almighty – then one knows that everything is God himself. All that we can see is not the world but God himself. *The Shankaracharya*

"The universe is a manifestation of the Absolute, and everything in it a manifestation of God's qualities; and the quality of God is not separated from his personality. The qualities of God, unseparated from each other, are in the Knowledge of God. In the world of manifestation, everything will be the thing it is meant to be; it is manifested like that. This ability of Being is the manifestation of the quality of God. In this universe the things which appear opposite to each other are nothing but the coming face to face of the variable qualities of God. In reality, this world is the world

of opposites, but from this multiplicity of opposites a harmony and unity appears." *Resuhi Baykara*

"In that world there can be none of the duality of our world. Being is not opposed to non-being; life is not opposed to death. The one includes the other. Unity and multiplicity, motion and immobility, oneness and divisibility, good and evil, truth and falsehood – all these divisions are impossible there. Everything subjective is objective, and everything objective is subjective. That world is the unity of opposites. That world and our world are not two different worlds. The world is one. That which we call our world is only our incorrect representation, the world seen through a narrow slit. As we begin to feel the reality and miraculous quality of that other world, our earthly world begins to appear unreal.[2]" *P.D. Ouspensky*

"The general concept of the coarse world and the subtle world which is known to common people, is that the coarse body is the biggest body, inside which is the subtle body, and smaller than the subtle body is the causal body. And within that small causal body is the Atman hiding in a remote corner.

But the reality is quite different on individual and universal levels – both. The coarse world is the smallest of all and surrounded by the extensive subtle world which again is merged into an extensive sphere of the causal world, and then everything is covered by the Atman which has no limits and no division." *The Shankaracharya*

Commentary on "And He is with you wheresoever ye be."

Once more we come back to the tale: when, indeed, did we go forth from the tale?

If we come to ignorance, that is His prison, and if we come to knowledge, that is His palace;

And if we come to sleep, we are His intoxicated ones; and if to wakefulness, we are in His hands;

And if we weep, we are a cloud laden with the bounty dis-

pensed by Him: and if we laugh, at that time we are His lightning;

And if (we come) to wrath and war, 'tis the reflexion of His Might; and if to peace and forgiveness, 'tis the reflexion of His Love.

Who are we? In this tangled (complex) world what (thing other than He) indeed hath He (who is single) like alif? Nothing, nothing.[3] *Rumi*

Part Three

THE PRACTICAL IMPLICATIONS OF THE FOUR LEVELS

Who Am I?

Throughout our lives we have all had a sense of an unchanging sense of 'I' that always remains the same regardless of changing interests and physical appearance. It's not the part of us that thinks or feels or reacts to life's events, or a part we can separate from and observe, but rather it feels much more like the basic sense of 'I' that itself stands in the background and observes and witnesses all the changes of mood and interest that go on within our psychology and the changing situations and fortunes that go on within our lives, yet all without comment and judgement.

It can be helpful to ask the question, "Who am I?" to find out with which level we identify our sense of self. For many the sense of identity is centred on the physical body but is this really the source of a permanent feeling of 'I' since it is constantly changing? My physical appearance at the age of five is totally different to my appearance at the age of fifty. Parts of my body may be removed or fall off naturally and eventually it will return back to the elements from which it came. Is this really a permanent sense of identity?

It is also very usual to identify our sense of self with the subtle body or psyche. If we observe this level closely and try to find a separate self it can't be done. All we find is a great emptiness as if there is no-one there. There is a surface display of ever-changing thoughts and desires which come and go like a varied cast of theatrical characters, but when we look beyond them there is no permanent separate entity or ego. This discovery can come as quite a surprise.

It is the same with the causal body. It may be the realm in which the light of pure Consciousness is reflected in the individual but that reflection appears to vary due to the degree of transparency or opacity and so, again, it cannot be said to be the ultimate source of a permanent sense of identity.

At the Divine level there is no feeling of change. It is always that same still presence. The times when we are aware of this level may vary but that is due to the changing nature of the other levels. This level is the ultimate source of our sense of 'I'. We tend to miss it simply because it is who we already are. We cannot search for it since it is already the subject, and we can only 'find' an object. This level is already quietly observing the fluctuations of our lives and our natures and yet it is our ultimate identity that never changes.

If this is who we already are then there is nothing to search for. It is more a question of realising 'what we are not'. It has only been missed because we have identified our sense of self with just a part of the whole, with the vehicle of Consciousness. From this view we are not all separate entities but are all aspects of the One Consciousness meeting itSelf and interacting with itSelf.

We don't have to find, create or even uncover this identity since it is already fully present as our own basic awareness, whether we know it or not. All that is necessary is to transfer our identity from what is seen to that which is already doing the seeing. This is only an acknowledgement of what is already happening, of that which already is.

As we become aware that our true identity is the witness of experience rather than the experience itself, we begin to see our mind/body mechanism as an object to observe rather than as the centre of our identity. When we identify our sense of self with anything that can be observed then we are subject to time and change and the dualities of birth and death, past and future, good and bad etc. This is what Joseph Campbell called, "The tick of time which shuts out the knowledge of eternity." When we withdraw our identification with what can be observed and acknowledge the witness, then we move beyond the field of time and into the 'Eternal Now'.

To acknowledge our identity as the ever present witness, we go back through this spectrum of identity until all that is left is our own basic awareness, which is who we are and Reality all at once.

States of Consciousness

One of the ways we can give up these lesser levels of identity is through the practice of meditation. When we first sit down to meditate we can be aware of the sensations of the physical body. As these quieten, we then notice the turning thoughts, feelings and desires of the subtle realm. As these begin to settle down we notice that behind them is a realm of stillness and emptiness. This, in fact, is the part of us that is aware of the turning thoughts. It is always there, underlying all movement. Sometimes we can become completely absorbed in this level of stillness so that there are no longer any objects in our awareness. It is as if a projector is running but with no film. The light shines but there is no projected image and there is no longer any separate sense of existence or identity or time.

In the Advaita tradition this state is known as Samadhi. It is natural to enter the causal realm at night during deep sleep. Here there is no experience, identity or sense of passing time. It is from this deep level of rest that we are recharged for the following day's activities. This state is also available during our daytime activities. It occurs between one set of desires and another, when we can naturally come to rest in this state of still awareness.

As we become more aware of this deep causal level of stillness, life starts to look more and more like a play or dream. We are no longer so identified with the character we are playing. We become more aware that we are the stillness that is impartially watching the drama of life unfolding in the same way that we view a film at the cinema. This state has sometimes been called Self Consciousness or Self Remembering. You have realised your identity as the still impartial witness or Atman and are no longer solely identified with the mind/body mechanism.

Paradoxically as our identity goes inwards in stillness, it also goes outwards in empathy. As each level is transcended it is integrated and included, not rejected. We then start to see our environment and those around us as all part of one Self and all worthy of love and compassion.

For the Advaita tradition describes a second stage to the realisation of our true nature, that is called 'Turiya' or Enlightenment. We then discover that this true Self or Atman is not just the

Witness or Observer, but is also one with all that is witnessed, so that wherever we look we see only Consciousness, and this is the true Non-Dual perspective.

Perception

It is important to remember that Non-Duality is not a remote state that the Universe is evolving towards, rather it already is Non-Dual. One of the ways we can come closer to understanding this is by applying the model of four levels to our modes of perception. It is possible to view the same event in a very different way depending on which level we view it from.

Rumi writing in the Mathnawi tells the story of an ant that sees a pen writing on a piece of paper and he says to a fellow ant, "Isn't it wonderful that the pen can do this writing." Another slightly wiser ant says, "No, it is not the pen but the hand that holds it." And another ant says, "No, it is not the hand but the arm that moves." And so the ants go back in the chain of causation, until one ant who is very wise says, "No, the writing is caused by the Universal Spirit that gives movement to all things."

This story illustrates how we tend to judge phenomena from a very narrow view point. Often we just take the physical or subtle level view in isolation and then form opinions based on this limited perspective but without seeing them in the context of the whole. The whole is the Divine level perspective. The terms 'physical' or 'subtle' are just metaphors for a partial understanding of the whole and, as such, they do not have any reality in themselves. The Reality is that we already are the Divine level, the other levels just exist within us or within our awareness.

We must all have examples from our lives of events which at the time appeared to be disasters, but when viewed from a fuller perspective were seen to be blessings. It was this sort of understanding that led Sir Laurens van der Post to suggest that we have to learn to trust our bad luck as much as our good luck as it's all part of the same thing. This is an example of how many of life's dualities lose their reality when seen from a fuller perspective. So we can trust the process of life's unfolding and we can trust that, like the man from Baghdad, we are all the time being shown, that we already possess a great treasure.

Quotations

"Then I began to hear the other voice, which came as it were from above, from a certain point above my head. I understood then that the whole problem and the whole object consisted in being able to hear this voice constantly, in being in constant communication with it. The being to whom this voice belonged knew everything, understood everything above all was free from thousands of small distracting 'personal' thoughts and moods. He could take everything calmly, could take everything objectively, as it was in reality. And at the same time this was I."[40]

P.D. Ouspensky

"What am I? Am I the bulb that carries the light, or am I the light of which the bulb is a vehicle?

One of the psychological problems in growing old is the fear of death. People resist the door of death. But this body is a vehicle of consciousness and if you can identify with the consciousness, you can watch this body go like an old car. There goes the fender, there goes the tyre, one thing after another, but it's predictable. And then, gradually the whole thing drops off, and consciousness rejoins consciousness."[1]

Joseph Campbell

"Don't think saying, "I am God" is proclaiming one's greatness, it is actually total humility. Someone who says, "I am the servant of God" infers two – God and himself, whereas someone who says, "I am God" negates himself, he relinquishes his own existence. "I am God" means I don't exist, everything is God, only God exists, I am nothing, I am utter emptiness. This is complete humility not arrogance, but people often misunderstand. When someone says he is God's servant he still sees himself as a doer, albeit in God's service, he is not yet drowned in the Ocean of God. When he is, there will be no such thing as his actions, only movements of the water." *Rumi*

"Man has become more and more separated from the

Source of Creation and has to find his way back. That is what all methods are designed for, the cornerstone is that he has to become the Observer. The eyes, for instance, could not observe for themselves, they need sensory organisation. The sensory organisation observed the eyes and is in turn observed by the intellect that tells it what it sees – the meaning, but the intellect in turn is observed by the Atman. It is only the Atman which is not observed by anything else. So when a man reaches the Ultimate Observer he reaches the Atman who just watches what goes on without becoming involved. *The Shankaracharya*

"His disciples said to Him, when will the Kingdom come? Jesus said, "It will not come by waiting for it. It will not be a matter of saying "Here it is" or "There it is". Rather, the Kingdom of the Father is spread out upon the Earth, and men do not see it." [4] *The Gospel of Thomas*

"The 'other world' is this world rightly seen."[5]
Ken Wilber

"If you begin to be what you are, you will realise everything, but to begin to be what you are, you must come out of what you are not. You are not those thoughts which are turning, turning in your mind; you are not those changing feelings; you are not the different decisions you make and the different wills you have; you are not that separate ego. Well then, what are you? You will find when you come out of what you are not, that the ripple on the water is whispering to you 'I am That', the birds in the trees are singing to you 'I am That', the moon and the stars are shining beacons to you 'I am That'. You are in everything in the world and everything in the world is reflected in you, and at the same time you are That – everything." *The Shankaracharya.*

Part Four

THE ANTAHKARANA

The Antahkarana is the 'inner vehicle' that comprises the causal and subtle level of an individual. It is the mechanism through which Consciousness manifests. In the early Christian terminology it could be equated with the 'soul', as it is the intermediary between the physical world on the one hand and the pure unmanifest Consciousness on the other.

It is important when looking at the mechanics of the Antahkarana that we do not lose sight of the One Consciousness, for which it is the vehicle, and which ultimately it manifests.

Let us look first at the causal level of the Antahkarana. It is the realm in which the separate functions of mind exist in unmanifest form as a single unit. It is also at this level that the seeds of both our individuality and our diversity are found, and this is in part due to our 'samskara' or 'essence' and the three gunas.

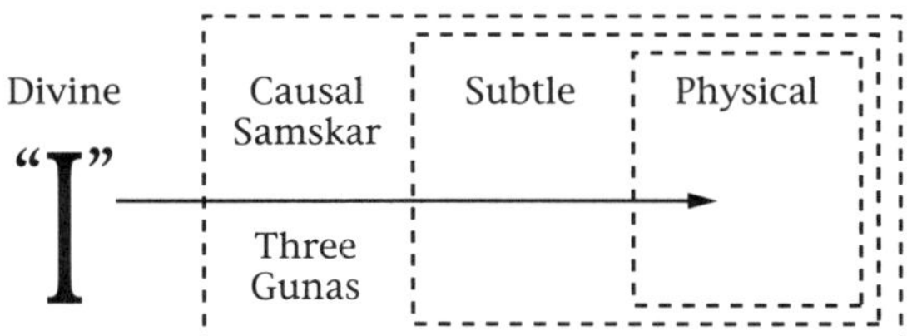

Samskara

We have seen how an individual's blue print and potential is stored at the causal level in unmanifest form. Samskara refers to that aspect of it that is built up by the repetition of desires and tendencies. This creates a coloured film through which the light of Consciousness is filtered, so that all we experience at the subtle level is influenced by this colour. This includes the way in which we perceive the outside world; whether we see it as it is, or if we see it as an extension of our own limited sense of self.

While samskara may, on the one hand, appear to obscure the light of our true Selves, it does on the other hand give us much of our individual colour, and so can also be seen as the grist to the mill in our life's journey of Self discovery.

In the Advaita tradition two methods are recommended for the purification of samskara and the removal of deep seated tendencies.

One method is the same way that the tendencies got there in the first place and that is repetition. We substitute outlived attitudes with new ones until they become part of our nature. The other method is through cultivating stillness so that our unwanted samskara is dissolved by the light of Consciousness. This tends to happen naturally. Outlived tendencies tend to fall away once they have fulfilled their function in our lives.

There is a further point, and that is avoiding creating further samskara. This comes about when we realise we really are just the actors in a drama, then we do what is necessary in each moment and let go of the results, for these belong to the One Consciousness of which we are all a part.

The Three Gunas

The Advaita tradition describes three forces or gunas that exist in the manifest creation. These give rise to all the multiplicity and diversity within creation. In our individual psyches we experience these as three types of energy: rajas, tamas and sattva. They work together like the different pedals and gears of a car.

Tamas is the passive guna of inertia. We need it for sleep at night and to slow us down during the day. Without it we would (and often do) burn ourselves out through lack of sufficient rest.

Rajas is the active guna, and we need it to motivate ourselves for our day's activity.

We often meet people who are predominately rajasic or tamasic in their natures. Or we ourselves often oscillate between the two; when we are very tamasic the world can look dark and fearful and we may be full of self pity. Or when we are rajasic we can be bossy and domineering with the 'my way is the only way' sort of attitude.

The third guna, 'sattva', is different and is not found so frequently in daily life. It is derived from the Sanskrit word 'sat' which means 'I am', so it is literally the 'Energy of Being'. It is a very still, creative energy that brings with it a deep feeling of quiet inner happiness. We often experience it after we have meditated, or done some activity with full attention, or done something for somebody else. Once we have the taste for it, it can be derived from so many different situations, from nature, from music, from art, from people. Often it wells up during the day when we least expect it, always giving that same quiet inner warmth and contentment.

When someone has an abundance of sattva all those around feel it too. Certain buildings and places also become saturated with it.

When the Antahkarana is predominately sattvic it becomes transparent like a clear glass. Then the light of Consciousness can flow straight through and we just become transparent vehicles for this deep sense of 'I AM'.

And yet it is important not to either hanker after or resent the presence of a particular guna, but just to quietly witness their ever-changing play.

The Four Functions

At the subtle level the Antahkarana is divided up into four separate functions which are referred to as manas, chitta, buddhi and Ahamkara.

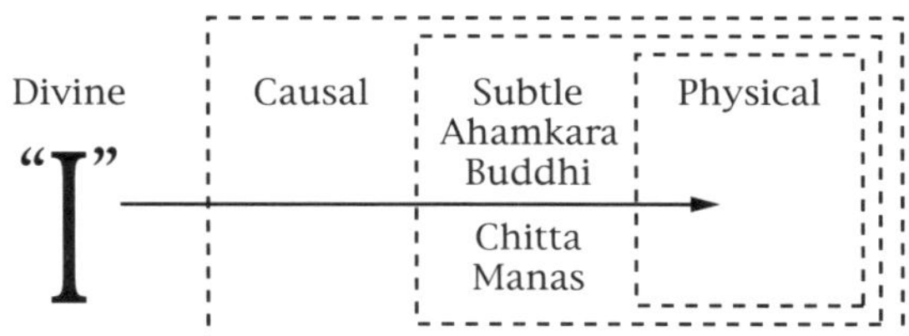

Manas is described as the registering and the desiring mind. Its job is to gather impressions from the outside world.

Chitta is the store of memory and the holder of knowledge. One of its jobs is to maintain the individual on a particular course in life.

The two functions that are said to be most important in Self Realisation are ahamkara and buddhi.

Ahamkara is our sense of I. 'Aham' in Sanskrit means 'I' and 'kar' means 'vehicle', so it is literally the 'vehicle for our sense of I'. As we have seen our sense of identity can be quite narrow if we just identify with the physical and subtle levels as separate entities, in which case it is known as 'false ahamkara'. Or we can identity our sense of self with the more limitless causal and divine levels, in which case it is 'true ahamkara'. So there exists a spectrum of levels of identity, from the separate physical body, through the psyche and the causal witness, to an identity with the whole universe at the divine level.

Buddhi is the organ of discrimination. On a day to day level it says 'yes' or 'no' in relation to the incoming impressions from manas. When it is working properly it keeps the desiring aspect of manas in check, so that we only desire those things that are really useful to the whole of our being. Buddhi also files the useful incoming impressions in the memory store (chitta) and is able to retrieve them when they are needed.

In relation to Self Realisation, buddhi's function of discrimination is known as 'viveka'. It is to remind us in the first place that we are not just the body, nor just the psyche, but the Atman. So it is buddhi that reminds us of who we really are. The root word 'budh' means 'to regain consciousness after a swoon'. Buddhi wakes us up to our true identity. It is a lovely feeling of release, like waking up from a bad dream, or coming back to one's true home. So having established our true inner identity, buddhi's job is then to remind us that the Atman is not just inside us, but is manifesting in everything we encounter.

The different functions also have universal aspects. When the Antahkarana is under the influence of sattva, we automatically give up our unreal identification with the mind/body mechanism. Then buddhi reflects the One Universal Discrimination, chitta reflects the Universal Knowledge, ahamkara stands for the

Universal Self or Param Atman and all our thoughts, feelings and actions arise from stillness and Universality.

Quotations

The following eleven quotations are from 'The Shankaracharya':

> *"The states of consciousness which we experience are governed by the influx of Sattva, Rajas and Tamas in people, places, situations and events.*
>
> *These all undergo change, but the Observer who sees them all as a passing show, always remains the same."*
>
> *"The Antahkarana is like a mirror, which on account of the dust of ignorance covering it, has stopped showing things clearly. Thus the Antahkarana is unable to show up the Atman in its pure form. Holy intentions, holy thoughts and holy actions remove the dirt of ignorance. Then the difference between Atman and Param Atman vanishes."*
>
> *"If a mirror is covered with dirt you will not be able to see your face as it actually is. On account of our past Samskar the mirror of our mind has become dirty, so we are not able to see the picture of Atman correctly."*
>
> *"If a glass is clean, then the sunlight can come through that glass without any invitation being offered to it, but the sunlight cannot penetrate if its sides are opaque and coated with mud."*
>
> *"The power, though unlimited, is obstructed by virtue of the previous tendencies. Just as sunlight is pervading the earth, a small cloud appears and obstructs that light."*
>
> *"If you take a mirror you see the image of your face. The common man considers in his ignorance that the image is the real thing. This is one of the illusions – the other factor is the dust or colour which lies on the mirror. Whatever dust*

or colour is on the mirror will obscure or colour the reflection of the face, which will look ugly or distorted. In fact the face within is never ugly. So the Light of the Atman reflected in the causal level of Antahkarana is pure, and yet because of the contamination of the Antahkarana due to gunas, you see things and people in varying colours. The only way to remove the dust and false colour from the mirror is to understand that the image is illusory but the face is real; only the light of pure Reason, the viveka, can help to remove both these illusions."

"The Ahankara part of the Antahkarana is responsible for this distinction between the observer and the object being observed. But when there is no Ahankara – there is only one – and there is no distinction between observer and the observed. A person asked a realised person – a sage – that when one Atman which is pure and absolute is pervading everywhere, then where is the need for any practice of Sadhana, because Atman is pure and is pervading everywhere. Why this Sadhana? What for? The sage replied that only by Sadhana you will be able to realise that this is pure and is pervading everywhere."

"The basic nature is pervading everything, and once you start experiencing it in all things then you will be able to enjoy it whatever your circumstance; so the main use of the intellect (Buddhi) is that it should be used in seeing, observing and feeling the all-pervasiveness of that perfect nature – just as when you see a tree your Buddhi should be able to convey to you that the basic nature which is in you is also in the tree.

It is another matter that this basic nature is making its appearance in different forms. In a creeper it is tender, in a stone it is hard, in the leaves of the tree it is green , in the individual it is in another form. The form may be different but the basic nature is the same. So when your Buddhi sees or appreciates this fact of the all-pervasiveness of nature, then in your everyday life, your normal duties, you will be able to enjoy the circumstances in which you are placed."

"Chit is like the sun, the real source of light, and Chitta is only a mirror, which merely reflects it, and from which the body, the mind, change under the influence of sensations arising in our consciousness."

"This changeability of the Chitta is due to its false sense of ownership over, or association with, the sensations in question."

"There is a Cosmic Chitta, Cosmic Buddhi and there is individualised Chitta and Buddhi. The substance is the same, but because we have certain influences in our essence they form a sheath around it; due to these sheaths we find impurity and movement in Chitta and Buddhi. Once they are cleaned and stilled one would see everything without being involved in it. One would see things as they are."

"If you could get rid of yourself just once, the Secret of Secrets would open to you.
The face of the unknown hidden beyond the universe would appear on the mirror of your perception." *Rumi*

Part Five

IMMANENCE

Sat Chit Ananda

We have talked quite a lot about the Universal Consciousness and the Atman, but what is the nature of this Universal Self? How can we recognise its voice? What is its taste?

According to the Advaita system the nature of the Universal Self has three qualities known as: sat, chit and ananda.

Sat, as we have seen earlier, means 'I am'. It is also sometimes translated as 'Being' or 'Truth'. Chit means Consciousness and Ananda is happiness or bliss.

We saw in the Antahkarana how we limit the capacity of each function by claiming the knowledge and experience as our own. Whereas when we acknowledge the true source each function reflects the Universal. So our capacity to experience the qualities of sat, chit and ananda is limited by mistakenly identifying our sense of self with just the vehicle. Or to put it very simply, when we acknowledge (chit) our true 'I Am' (sat) we experience an unconditional happiness (ananda).

We are able to use these three qualities as guides to our true Being. Joseph Campbell said that he came to his idea of 'following your bliss' because of the concept of sat chit ananda. He said that he didn't know if his consciousness was true Consciousness, nor if his being was true Being but he knew where his rapture or happiness was and by following that deep sense of rightness, it led him to the other two qualities.

It is important to remember that this unconditional happiness or ananda that suddenly emerges from within, often regardless of circumstance, is one of the properties of our true Selves. When this happens we start to see all our other experiences of happiness as reflections or dim memories of this one Great Happiness. We may think that we are experiencing happiness as a result of people, places, objects and events but what we are really experiencing is the one Self reflected in all these forms. These forms are all pointers to this Reality. They each serve as a reminder of its existence and, like a paper trail, can lead us back from form to a formless state. In this way we may find ourselves overwhelmed with a great happiness when we hear a piece of music we love or see a painting, a landscape, a person or an animal. They all point to the great Source which they are manifesting and reflecting.

Immanence and Transcendence

In the world's mystical traditions there exist two approaches to Consciousness that can sometimes appear contradictory, but which in a true Non Dual model are seen to be both aspects of the same thing.

On the one hand we have heard that Consciousness is available right now, manifesting appropriately in everything we encounter and on the other hand that Consciousness is experienced only as a result of persistent systematic practice. How can we reconcile these two views?

In the Advaita teaching we are told of two different approaches. The first is for the 'purpose of training', while the second is the Reality. Both are necessary.

In the first approach, because we mistakenly believe that we are separate beings living in a world of multiplicity, certain metaphors and practices are used to correct our viewpoint since just to be told that everything is the Universal Consciousness is usually not enough. Because we tend not to believe it, or only believe it sometimes, and with a very small part of our whole being, as it requires turning around some very deep rooted views and tendencies.

So in the first stage we are advised to use our discrimination to gradually shed our identity with the outer world of manifestation. This can be easily observed in the process of meditation. At first we let go of our identity with physical sensations and sense perceptions. Having done that we then become aware of the internal voices of thoughts and desires. By attending to the mantra this level too can gradually be transcended, until the mantra itself loses it physical sound and becomes just a pulse, and then in deep stillness just a presence.

This is an example of finding our own true Self or inner Reality by a process of transcendence. We are using our discriminative mind to transcend lesser levels of identity, until we find that which is timeless and unchanging at the centre of our being.

As we continue to practice this process of transcendence, it gradually becomes second nature to identify our sense of self with this still silent witness. The ups and downs of our daily lives no longer have quite the power they once did to overwhelm us.

However, if we stop at this stage, we are still to a certain extent in a world of duality. We may have identified with our pure witnessing awareness, but there is still an outer world to be witnessed. There is still the duality of subject and object, the seer and the seen.

The second stage involves realising that Reality is not just transcendent, but it is also immanent. So where in the first stage we gradually disengaged our identity with the world of phenomena, in the second stage we discover that Consciousness is not only who we are, but immanent and present in everything and every situation that we encounter. So part of this practice is to constantly remind ourselves of this fact.

These two approaches are demonstrated in a practical way, in the Buddhist concept of Wisdom and Compassion. Wisdom is the effort by the discriminative mind to return to its source, while compassion is the outflowing from that source of itSelf into all creation.

Compassion is also the practical outcome of the realisation that we are all one, and what we do to another we do to ourSelf. Just as the Christian instruction to love our neighbour as our Self becomes a matter of fact, since our neighbour is our Self.

Bhakti and Surrender

We have seen in our study of the four levels and the Antahkarana that when we give up our limited identity as just a mind body mechanism, that we become aware of a much larger identity.

There exists a very direct and practical route to this realisation and that is through the Shankaracharya's teaching on Bhakti and Surrender.

Bhakti is the way of love and devotion and is ideally suited to the householder, since we are not required to change our lives but only our attitude to them. By this way our daily activities are no longer done solely for ourselves as separate entities but are dedicated to the Universal Self, and whatever happens to us is also seen as coming from this same Universal Self.

We do our best at each moment with the energy and circumstances available to us, and then give up the result to the Universal. This way we start to experience ourselves as part of a great unfolding, and no longer as a small separate self, manipulating a separate external world.

When we practise surrender, we merge our own individual will with the One Universal Will, and do not make grievances if events do not always unfold in the way our separate ego self may have intended.

One of the ways we can come closer to understanding this is to look at our own lives. Often it is possible to see a pattern in the way events unfold. There are far too many coincidences to be accounted for by accident: meeting people at just the right time, the way a book may fall into our hands expressing just what we need to know, a friend ringing or turning up just when they are needed.

Another way of understanding this is when things don't happen. We often set our heart on a particular objective in life; it might be a person or a job or a house and, despite our best efforts, events will not unfold in the way we want. Later we see the reason for that; the person, job or house turns out to be totally unsuitable in a way we could not foresee, and something that is much more suited to our needs emerges unexpectedly in its own time, as if it was quietly waiting for us to be ready for it. As Rumi puts it in the Mathnawi:

> Don't grieve for what doesn't come,
> some things that don't happen
> keep disasters from happening

When we observe this pattern, it can feel as if we are being looked after in a way we never expected. This can then lead us to trust the Universal and trust the process of life's unfolding. Then love and gratitude often arise spontaneously. All of life provides the means for this realisation, no matter what our particular circumstances or life situation, and it is often the case that the more adverse our circumstances, the greater is the capacity and potential for transformation. For it is in difficult times, when we cannot see our way through a particular situation, that we are brought to the point of surrender and say, 'Thy Will be done', when we unexpectedly open up to the Universal.

So with the practice of Bhakti our view of life becomes very different and we start to see that we are always being presented with the best thing possible for this journey of Self-discovery. In playing our own role in life, whatever it may be, and not wanting this moment to be other than it already is, we see that we are truly already that which we are seeking.

Quotations

The following six quotations are all from 'The Shankaracharya':

> *"Ananda is the natural state of the Atman when all other things and obstacles are removed, then the Atman exists in the Ananda; no-one in the Creation can exist without some Ananda. One might feel that as one develops on the Way and makes progress, so one feels that Ananda is also improving or developing, but this is only illusory. The real state is that Ananda is always with the Atman and so unchanging. It is only our view of it which has changed."*

> *"In our discipline two processes are adopted – as previously described one of Vyatireka and the other is Anvaya. Anvaya follows Vyatireka, so any person who is being disciplined and put on the Way is first given Vyatireka. By this discipline one simply segregates everything which is non-Self, and this is done only to establish the authority and existence of the Self.*

> *Having established the authority and existence of the Self which is not seen by any sensory medium, then it is also necessary for this system to go through the Anvaya process to establish the unity of the whole Creation. Otherwise, hav-*

ing separated the Self from the non-Self it leaves some scope for duality to dwell, and this duality must be annihilated, and this is done through Anvaya, which means that everything one comes across in this Creation is a manifestation of the same Self whose authority has been established. Neither in knowledge, nor in action, nor in experience should duality come."

"According to us today, the need for all of us is to understand and explain the Absolute, or Param Atman, who is immanent, always present, together with us, guiding and helping at each moment in every walk of life."

"The method is, do what each of you is meant for, and do it in a spirit of service to God. Let eating, drinking, sleeping, bathing etc., all be dedicated to God. This is the correct worship, and the correct Bhakti."

"It should be understood here that that so-called 'devotion' (which we can attempt before acquaintance), is a forced phenomenon and unreal, while that which sets in inevitably after acquaintance, is real. Then our body, mind and all the possessions become dedicated to Param Atman, and this dedication itself becomes the worship of Param Atman. Then we eat, drink, act, etc. for the sake of Param Atman and do nothing for ourselves. Everywhere and in everything we see nothing but Param Atman. This is a stage of absolute intimacy with Param Atman, and Bhakti is just another word for this stage."

"The only thing that is getting in our way, between us and the Atman, is the usurper, the usurping part of us, the imaginary part, which says, 'I am doing everything. I am bad. I am good. I will go to heaven. I will go to hell.' Everything that says I is complete fiction; there is no such I. It's some other actor in the repertoire of the company talking for you and calling himself 'I'." *Dr Roles*

"But is God really the doer of all the actions I perform? The

present difficulty is that man thinks he is the doer. But it is a mistake. It is the higher power which does everything and man is only a tool. If he accepts that position, he is free from troubles, otherwise he courts them. Take, for instance, the sculpted figure at the base a gopuram (temple tower), which is made to appear as if it is bearing the burden of the tower on its shoulder. Its posture and look are a picture of great strain which gives the impression that it is bearing the weight of the tower. But think. The tower is built on the earth and rests on its foundations. The figure is a part of the tower, but it is made to look as if it is bearing the weight of the tower. Is it not funny? So also is the man who takes on himself the sense of doing." *Ramana Maharshi*

"The gloom of the world is but a shadow. Behind it, yet within our reach, is joy. There is radiance and glory in the darkness, could we but see; and to see, we have only to look. I beseech you to look.

Life is so generous a giver, but we, judging its gifts by their covering, cast them away as ugly or heavy or hard. Remove the covering, and you will find beneath it a living splendour, woven of love, by wisdom, with power. Welcome it, grasp it and you touch the Angel's hand that brings it to you. Everything we call a trial, a sorrow, or a duty: believe me, that angel's hand is there; the gift is there, and the wonder of an overshadowing presence. Our joys too; be not content with them as joys, they too conceal diviner gifts.

Life is so full of meaning and of purpose, so full of beauty – beneath its covering – that you will find that earth but cloaks your heaven. Courage, then to claim it: that is all! But courage you have, and the knowledge that we are pilgrims together, wending through unknown country, home."

Fra Giovanni

"When you work with Wu Wei, you put the round peg in the round hole and the square peg in the square hole. No stress, no struggle. Egotistical Desire tries to force the round peg into the square hole and the square peg into the round hole. Cleverness tries to devise craftier ways of making pegs fit

where they don't belong. Knowledge tries to figure out why round pegs fit round holes, but not square holes. Wu Wei doesn't try. It doesn't think about it. It just does it. And when it does, it doesn't appear to do much of anything. But Things Get Done."[6] *Benjamin Hoff.*

"I don't know for what reasons I'm here, I've given up projecting into the future, I live in a state of non-expectation. Give up expecting everything of people, expecting everything of life, and life comes up with so many surprises ... There's nothing to win, nothing to prove, because of myself I can do nothing, and that's a state of surrender, of giving it over to the very force of life itself." *Anthony Hopkins*

"Trust in God but tie the knee of your camel."[3] *Rumi*

"We did not come to remain whole,
We came to lose our leaves like the trees,
The trees that are broken
And start again, drawing up from the great roots"[7]
Robert Bly

Part Six

BEING AND THE ETERNAL NOW

The seventeenth century philosopher, René Descartes, is well-known for his statement, "I think therefore I am". In saying this he tried to limit our identity to just the thinking aspect of the subtle body. However, this argument falls apart when we realise that there is a part of ourselves that is aware that we are thinking, that quietly witnesses the thinking and feeling processes. Clearly Consciousness is far more than just thought.

In the Book of Exodus in the Bible, God says to Moses from the midst of the burning bush, "I AM THAT I AM" and "I AM hath sent me unto you". In these statements there only the pure sense of 'Amness' without any qualification, that which is the same for each individual.

Our deepest identity is the feeling of 'I AM'. This feeling is universally felt by all living beings; it is our true identity that is beyond birth and death and beyond change. We saw in our study of the four levels how we tend to identify this with the vehicle of Consciousness rather than with the Consciousness itSelf. This is how our sense of 'I AM' becomes confused with our identity on the line of time in the drama of life. We start to qualify that identity not just by saying, "I AM" but by saying, "I am a man" or "I am a woman", "I am British", "I am Indian", "I am ten years old", "I am fifty years old", "I am a writer, a doctor, an artist" and so on. In taking on these lesser identities as to who we really are, we miss out on our one true identity that is always present and is beyond all change and suffering.

In many of the world's mystical traditions there exists the concept of 'Being'. In the Zen Buddhist traditions it is often called the 'Isness' of a thing or person. It is quite distinct from any identity in life, no matter how important, learned or respectable a person may be. Although it is hard to explain, there are some people who appear to have much more of a sense of 'Being' or 'Isness' or 'Presence' than others. They may be quite old or frail and yet something seems to radiate out of them; there is a quality of light, warmth, humour and good nature. Being in the company of such people brings about that same feeling in oneself. The moving mind with all its concerns starts to lose its grip and suddenly everything seems to be alright.

This quality of Being is not only unique to great saints and teachers but can also be found in the most unlikely people in perfectly ordinary circumstances. Often this quality is seen in people not long before they die. As daily life and its drama starts to lose its importance, this underlying identity starts to shine through.

'Being' could be described as the degree to which we are aware of our true identity as this unchanging sense of 'I AM', that which is total stillness and total emptiness. When our identity is concerned only with the line of time, this quality is missed except for occasional glimpses. Awareness of our true Being gives a feeling of becoming transparent as the time-bound identity starts to appear more and more illusory. There is an awareness of a great impersonal force that flows through one and outwards as if one is just a vehicle and, at the same time, this is who one is.

One of the keys to the experience of our true Being or sense of 'I AM' is that is doesn't exist in time. When we live only with our sense of identity which is on the line of time, we are always caught up in the past or the future, neither of which actually exist. However, it does not mean that it is completely true to say that this sense of 'I AM' only exists in the present moment, since that too is another aspect of time, when time is a mind-made concept or another metaphor. Perhaps it is more accurate to say that there is always "just this" which gives a feeling of being outside time altogether, a sense of eternity or the 'Eternal Now'.

Returning to the story of the man from Baghdad who dreamed of the great treasure in Cairo and who, after many adventures, returned to find the treasure in his own house in Baghdad, we can see that we are all rather like him. We know we have lost something yet we look for it on the line of passing time. Eventually we exhaust that search and come to the realisation that it does not lie in time at all, but only in the eternal now and that it is always available. So we discover that the treasure was always in our own house all the time.

The process of life eventually provides this realisation because when we are very happy we find ourselves automatically in the present, wanting this moment never to end. And when life is difficult, silently resting in the present and not allowing the mind to move forward or back can often be our only refuge. Fear about the future and regret and anger about the past only exist if we let our minds move away from the present. When we meet the anticipated future event it is met in the light of the present and that is usually very different from the way we imagined it.

As Winston Churchill once quoted an old man as saying on his death bed, "I've had a lot of trouble in my life most of which never happened."

When we silently rest in the present our connection with a separate self, supported by the memory of passing time, dissolves and we become aware of a much larger presence that exists only in the now. So it appears that we are leaving our home and making a journey but in reality we never ever leave our true home, for it is always with us and available in the present.

Quotations

> *"The present moment is the immanent Absolute, and in the present moment He comes in His form in front of everyone and that is the moment for everyone to appreciate the Absolute. The concept of past and future is involved with worldly affairs, so, when one thinks of the past, one is deviating from the Absolute which is present, and one is trying to have certain relationships with worldly things. When one is planning about the future, then one is deviating from the present Absolute."* — *The Shankaracharya*

> *"The present is always lit, because it is the presence of the Absolute, and the light of the Absolute falls on the present. There is nothing to worry about or fear in the present. Past and future are very dark, and that is where the fears are, and it is only fears of some sort which drag individuals to the past or the future. It is much better and more economical for us to avail ourselves of the brilliance and the light and knowledge which are of the present, and not to associate ourselves with the darkness which really belongs to the past*

or the future. They visit us, and concern us sometimes. Whenever we wake up and find that we are travelling towards the darkness of the past or future, please come into the light of the day – the light of the present."

The Shankaracharya

"A man had to travel ten miles away to attend to some urgent work. It was late at night and very dark. He took his lantern and came out of the house. He looked out and saw that pitch darkness prevailed the whole ten miles to his destination. He thought of his small lantern and wondered how he could find his way through the darkness. Fortunately, a holy man passed by and he enquired why the man was pausing at the threshold. The man expressed his fear of travelling ten miles with a light which only shone ten feet. The holy man told him not to worry because the moment he stepped forward, the light would also move forward. The light would always be ten feet ahead of him, so he should not worry, just proceed. So he did, and reached his destination." *The Shankaracharya*

"These roses under my window make no reference to former roses or to better ones; they are for what they are; they exist with God today. There is no time for them. There is simply the rose; it is perfect in every moment of its existence ... But man postpones or remembers; he does not live in the present, but with reverted eye laments the past, or heedless of the riches that surround him, stands on tiptoe to foresee the future. He cannot be happy and strong until he too lives with nature in the present above time." *Emerson*

" 'Have you,' he once asked him, 'have you also learnt that secret from the river – the secret that there is no time?'

A radiant smile spread over Vasudeva's face. 'Yes, Siddhartha,' he said. 'That is surely what you mean when you say that the river is everywhere at once, at its source and at its mouth, at the waterfall, at the ferry, at the rapids, at the sea, in the mountains – everywhere at once. And that there is for it only the present, not the shadow of the past, nor the shadow of the future.'

'That is so,' said Siddhartha. 'And when I had learnt it I looked at my life, and it too was a river, and the boy Siddhartha was separated from the man Siddhartha and from the aged Siddhartha only by shadows, not by anything real. Even Siddhartha's earlier incarnations were not past, and his death and his return to Brahma not future. Nothing was, nothing will be: everything is, everything has being, everything has presence.'"[8] *Herman Hesse*

"Eternity isn't some later time. Eternity isn't even a long time. Eternity has nothing to do with time. Eternity is that dimension of here and now that all thinking in temporal terms cuts off. And if you don't get it here, you won't get it anywhere. The experience of eternity right here and now, in all things, whether thought of as good or as evil, is the function of Life."[1] *Joseph Campbell*

Part Seven

THE LADDER OF SELF REALISATION

We have seen how we are already aspects of the One Universal Consciousness, yet we mistakenly perceive ourselves as being separate from each other and from the world. In the Non Dual traditions, because it is sometimes difficult to grasp this all at once, a series of metaphorical steps are employed to lead us from apparent duality into the realisation of our already existing Unity. Different systems employ different metaphors. In the Shankaracharya's tradition the ladder of Self Realisation is used.

It is important that we do not see this as a ladder to achieve something far away and remote. Rather it is a process of letting go of layers of mistaken identity and discovering who we already are. So it is not a process of addition but rather of subtraction, not of increased activity, but decreased activity and deeper levels of stillness and surrender.

Having reached a decision we start to see that help comes from all sorts of unexpected quarters and that all the help we need for this journey is provided. Then we understand that while it appears that we, as separate individuals, are making a journey from duality to unity, in reality all the impulses come from the Self. Just as the motivation and inspiration for effort comes from that Self, so it is really a matter of the Self unfolding itSelf to itSelf. For once we have the taste of this deep inner happiness no other happiness seems to fully satisfy us. Then we are led along, as the Shankaracharya says, like ants following a trail of sugar. As this process deepens we then start to see everything as aspects of one single unity, and concepts such as separation and independent existence start to lose their reality.

Quotations

"First Stage is the 'Good Intention', the 'Right Impulse', the arising of the right desire. This is the starting point which leads to

Second Stage: Decision: This is the stage where rationally (intellectually) the man makes up his mind and can go further. He has no doubt about the Way, which is in line with his intention and conviction.

Third Stage: Effort: Certain particles of fine matters have formed in the organism which causes him to strive toward Sattva.

Fourth Stage: Pull of the Way: Where influences from the Way pull him from the outside world of sensory impressions of pleasures or pain, so that these begin to lose some of their power.

Fifth Stage: Insight: which denotes that the man starts looking at himself and other things as they really are. He gets right values for everything; he realises about things what they are, how they are constituted and what their properties are.

Sixth Stage: Abundance, which is the stage where the outward pull is nearly gone, and he is filled with abundance of Sattva or Divine Love and happiness. The climax of this stage is Samadhi.

The last or Seventh Stage, which is called Turiya, is the stage of the fully Realised man, when he knows Himself; he knows all that can be known; he knows how to do, and whatever he does is just the right thing, right actions, right feeling, right thought – everything all combined. That is the Seventh Stage of the Seven-stage System of Nyaya for Self-Realisation."

The Shankaracharya

"Until one is committed, there is hesitancy, the chance to draw back, always ineffectiveness. Concerning all acts of initiative (and creation) there is one elementary truth, the ignorance of which kills countless ideas and splendid plans, that the moment one definitely commits oneself then Providence moves too.

All sorts of things occur to help one that would never otherwise have occurred. A whole stream of events issues from the decision, raising in one's favour all manner of unforeseen incidents and meetings and material assistance, which no man could have dreamed would have come his way.

Whatever you can do or dream, begin it. Boldness has genius, power and magic in it – Begin it now." *Goethe*

"There is one thing that many people have said to me, and I've felt very much myself; one sometimes counts the number of lucky accidents that seem to happen to one. One hasn't deserved them in any way, but one suddenly thinks, supposing that had gone the other way, where would I have been, and in fact these lucky accidents which come to meditators and people who are trying to realise their possibilities, increase and increase and increase and, of course, they aren't accidents at all. Has anybody felt this, that really these lucky accidents are totally undeserved, but how nice. That's another way of seeing a certain force pervading everything and to be picked up by anybody in a receptive state. It is all there, we've just got to be receptive."

Dr Roles

"In the alchemy of the heart everything is taken care of, and the process shapes itself as the devotee wants it to shape. Faith is the most important thing – faith in the unchanging Absolute, and faith in the meditation. One simply steadfastly keeps on going and in the course of time it will become natural and give the needed truth."

The Shankaracharya

"Work. Keep digging your well.
Don't think about getting off from work.
Water is there somewhere.

Submit to a daily practice.
Your loyalty to that
is a ring on the door.

Keep knocking, and the joy inside
will eventually open a window
and look out to see who's there." *Rumi*

"God is not found in the soul by adding anything but by a process of subtraction." *Meister Eckhart*

Part Eight

SANATANA DHARMA

Part of Self Realisation includes our action in the world, and playing our different roles in the unfolding drama of life. As people studying and practising the teaching of Non Dualism, part of our particular role in that drama is to manifest this teaching in our daily lives. One of the ways we are helped in this is through the teaching on Sanatana Dharma.

Sanatana Dharma means "body of Eternal religion" and its principles lie at the core of all religions. It is sometimes described as the religion of the Self or Atman. When we listen to the promptings coming from our own true Selves, we always have an innate sense of what is the right or wrong course of action to take in a given situation. So the principles of Sanatana Dharma outline how we would act from the point of view of the Non Dual perspective. They are a natural outcome of the realisation that we are all aspects of One Universal Consciousness.

For example, if we were to perceive ourselves as being separate individuals acting on a hostile external world, then it would be difficult to really have "confidence and patience". We are more likely to be unconfident and manipulative. But from a point of confidence born out of the Non Dual perspective, we are able to act appropriately as the occasions demand and then let go of the results and put our trust in the Universal.

Similarly, if we really perceive everybody as aspects of one whole, then it is difficult to be judgmental and apportion blame. This is because as our sense of separation dissolves, the concept of "others" to blame also dissolves. As Rumi suggests in the Mathnawi; the faults we see in others are usually aspects of our own characters projected. Once we see this, then having consideration for people's faults and providing space, follows naturally.

The concept of "non stealing" can be taken on many levels, for everything that we appear to "own" is really just on loan for a short time. And when we attribute our achievements, whether physical or psychological, to ourselves we are claiming what really belongs to the Universal who is the real "Doer".

Quotations

The following account of the ten principles of Sanatana Dharma is summarised from an account the Shankaracharya gave in 1989:

1. dhriti	*'spiritual patience, having confidence and patience.' If there is no confidence there can't be patience; the two are united, defined in the Sanskrit dictionary as "holding fast, standing still, firmness, fortitude, constancy, resoluteness, satisfaction, contentment."*
2. kshama	*'forgiveness, having consideration, giving pardon, being tolerant of the difficulties and faults of others, providing them with space.'*
3. dama	*'control of the outer senses,' every individual needs control over the sensory appetite and its expression, control over one's reactions to the messages and stimuli from external sources.*
4. asteya	*'non stealing'. The commentary: you should take only what you deserve and consider everyone else equally deserving. All that you accumulate extra is theft, theft from the Universe.*
5. saucha	*'internal and external purity.' One has to learn to clean one's body, one's mind and one's heart and for that one has to find a system through a teacher.*

6. indriya nigraha *'control of the inner senses.' There is a natural course of the use of the senses. One does not curb them but regulates them. The curbing of excessive use will then take place naturally. In the dictionary 'Indriya' means "the organ of sense" and 'Nigraha' means "restraint of the senses."*

7. dhee *'intuition, visualisation or imagination.' The intellect, reason or Buddhi, to find out the cause of things and to use them as the necessity may arise. And the definition in the dictionary of dhee is "a thought or conception, intuition, purpose, opinion, intelligence, insight."*

8. vidya *'knowledge through a process of meditation or worship.' One has to acquire true knowledge which is made manifest through the Vedas and is not man made. So acquire the knowledge of the Scriptures.*

9. satya *'the truth, Brahmin or the Absolute.' There is only one truth, there can't be two different truths. We should not deceive ourselves with our own brand of the truth.*

10. akrodha *'absence of anger'. One should never get agitated, taking a hard line is not necessarily getting agitated. Distinguish between right action and wrong agitation.*

"The mark of a moderate man is freedom from his own ideas. Tolerant like the sky, all-pervading like the sunlight, firm like a mountain, supple like a tree in the wind, he has no destination in view and makes use of anything life happens to bring his way."[17] *Tao Te Ching*

"Our deepest fear is that we are powerful, beyond measure.
It is our light, not our darkness that most frightens us.
We ask ourselves 'who am I to be brilliant, gorgeous, talented, fabulous?'
Actually who are you not to be?
You are a child of God. Your playing small does not serve the world. There's nothing enlightened about shrinking so that other people won't feel insecure around you.
We are all meant to shine as children do.
We were born to make manifest the glory of God that is within us. It's not just in some of us; it's in everyone.
And as we let our own light shine
We unconsciously give other people permission to do the same. As we are liberated from our own fear, our presence automatically liberates others."

Marianne Williamson
(Quoted by Nelson Mandela in his inaugural address)

"People are often unreasonable, illogical, and self-centred;
Forgive them anyway.
If you are kind, people will accuse you of selfish, ulterior motives;
Be kind anyway.
If you are successful, you will win some false friends and some true enemies;
Succeed anyway.
If you are honest and frank, people may cheat you;
Be honest and frank anyway.
What you spend years building, someone could destroy overnight;
Build anyway.
If you find serenity and happiness, they may be jealous;
Be happy anyway.

The good you do today, people will often forget tomorrow;
Do good anyway.
Give the world the best you have, and it may never be enough;
Give the world the best you've got anyway.
You see in the final analysis, it is between you and God;
It was never between you and them anyway."

(A handwritten note on the wall of Mother Theresa's room.)

Part Nine

AHAM – IDAM

One of the most practical aspects of the Advaita system in relation to Self Realisation is the teaching on Aham and Idam. Aham, as we have seen previously, means “I” whereas Idam means “That”. Aham represents the subject and Idam the object. For example, when we observe a landscape of sky, hills and trees we, as the observer, are the subject or Aham, but looking out through out eyes we can observe the landscape as something separate and external to us, as “That” or Idam.

“I” ——→ “THAT”
(AHAM) (IDAM)

As we shall see, it is a sliding scale for what we regard as subject and what we regard as object can change at different stages of our lives. The science of psychology tells us that when we are first born we do not differentiate ourselves from the world around us. Gradually, as we grow, we learn to separate ourselves from the world and other people. It is part of developing a mature ego that is necessary for functioning in life. So we arrive at the normal state where we identify with our mind/body mechanism as “I” or Aham and everything external to us as “That” or Idam. It is usual for us to see our physical bodies as separate objects and to say, “my leg is hurting” rather than “I'm hurting”. But then we may also say, “I'm feeling happy today” rather than “my psyche is feeling happy today”. This suggests that our sense of “I” is most commonly identified with the subtle level or psyche. When we do identify with just the mind/body mechanism we are very much at the mercy of life's changing fortunes. When life goes our way we are happy but when it does not, we are unhappy.

In the process of Self Realisation our centre of identity is gradually transferred back through the different levels so that we start to identify with the still, silent Witness at the Causal level. We then begin to see our mind/body mechanism as an object or a vehicle, no longer as the sole basis of our sense of identity so that, rather than being totally absorbed in the character we are playing, a part of us remains outside.

There is a further stage that the mystics describe. That is when our sense of identity shifts to the Divine level. Then there no longer exists the division into subject and object or Aham and Idam. For all is experienced as Aham or "I". There is no longer an Idam or external world. The universe is experienced as internal and all part of oneSelf. It is not a return to the pre-rational unity of the baby but rather it is a unity that both integrates and transcends rationality and is full of empathy for all creation.

The Five Veils

We saw in our study of Aham and Idam how our identity of self can be more or less limited and how there exists a sliding scale as to what we regard as subject and what we regard as object. The teaching of the five veils is a concept that first appeared in the Upanishads and was developed by the first Shri Shankara in his book that outlines the basis of the Advaita teaching: "The Crest Jewel of Wisdom".

The teaching describes how the Self or Atman is covered over by a series of veils from which we have to become detached, one after the other, so that the Self can be revealed in its purity as the sole Witness.

Again, it is a case of mistaken identity for the different levels only become veils to the Self when we identify with them as "I". Otherwise they are seen as part of the vehicle through which the Self is able to manifest in the world.

The first veil is the "anna maya" or food veil. It is the physical body of flesh and bones and its state can obviously have a very big influence on how we feel and how we view the world. For instance, when we experience physical pain, it can be helpful to step back and find a part of our being that is beyond the pain, and from which we can witness the physical sensations of the body. So we become aware of the physical body as a vehicle that is a part of us but no longer all of us. For we can witness its changing sensations from a point of stillness.

The next veil is the "prana maya" and relates to the various bodily rhythms, the neurochemical mechanisms, the glandular cycles, physical vitality or lack of it etc. It is still predominantly physical and can, for the most part, be measured by the physical sciences and yet its influence on our state of mind and our emotions is immense. Once we come to recognise its effects it comes as such a relief to no longer have to identify with it as self, but stand back and witness its changing cycles and changing moods.

The next two veils belong to the subtle realm of experience. The "mano maya" relates to the manas, the registering and desiring part of the mind. If unchecked it leads us away from seeing the depth of the present moment and into an imagined past or future. It is rarely satisfied with what is, but rather interprets events from its own limited viewpoint. It results in the distinction between I and other, for when we are in deep sleep and the manas is quiet, this distinction no longer exists.

The "vijnana maya" veil related to Buddhi, the function of discrimination. One of its roles is to remind us of who we really are but when it is under the influence of manas, it forgets this function and attributes its actions to itself and to the mind/body mechanism. So the vijnana maya veil is the basis of our mistaken sense of identity and our mistaken sense of doership. It forgets that the universe is the manifestation of the Universal Consciousness who is the real doer. When we acknowledge our identity as the Self or sole Witness then under its silent impartial gaze Buddhi resumes its function as the vehicle of the Self, and no longer considers itself a separate doer.

The final veil that lies at the threshold of the causal body is the "ananda maya" or veil of Bliss. It can seem strange that bliss is a veil but it is still an experience and subject to a beginning and an end. So it is still not the One who witnesses the experience.

Returning to the teaching of Aham and Idam, we see that when we identify with that which can be observed, then it is not our true Selves since it is subject to change. When we acknowledge our identity as the Witness of experience then we already are the unchanging stillness that knows no boundaries and is beyond birth and death.

Quotations

"As for the touch of Aham or taste of Aham – it is misunderstanding of the terms. Aham and Idam constitute this creation. Aham is Sat, Chit and Anand. Idam contains everything that reflects Sat, Chit and Anand through elements, essences, sensations, thinking and feeling. Aham is still, although it provides all the energies necessary for the Idam and its multifarious forms of this creation to exist, provides all sensations through the elements and their qualities, and all thinking and feeling. To know anything, or think about anything is to know and think of Idam. It is done by Aham. When one experiences the beauty of vision or the essence of the form and colour or touch and taste one can do so only from Idam. One never sees or touches or tastes the Aham. What one experiences is the bliss which is the being of Aham.

To be Aham is to be still. One can't touch it. Aham is beyond experience because it is the experiencer. The eyes see beauty, but who does really feel the bliss of beauty? Eyes are instruments and the real witness of beauty and bliss is the Aham, the Atman, which provides the power to see. If that force is missing eyes cannot see. They see through the light of the Atman. The same applies to all organs of senses, organs of action, and also the Antahkaran, with Manas, Buddhi, Chitta and Ahankar. They enjoy bliss from Idam because the bliss, the Atman, pervades everywhere. Consciousness pervades everywhere. Consciousness is not movement. Consciousness knows itself, and knows everything through these agencies. When it knows itself then no Idam will be there. It is all in stillness. So the taste of Aham or touch of Aham is a mistake in terms. It is existence, consciousness or bliss itself."

The Shankaracharya

"With the awakening of constant consciousness, you become something of a divine schizophrenic, in the popular sense of "split-minded," because you have access to both the Witness and the ego. You are actually "whole-minded", but it sounds like it's split, because you are aware of the constant Witness or Spirit in you, and you are also perfectly aware of the movie of life, the ego and all its ups and downs. So you still feel pain and suffering and sorrow, but they can no longer convince you of their importance – you are no longer the victim of life, but its Witness.

In fact, because you are no longer afraid of your feelings, you can engage them with much greater intensity. The movie of life becomes more vivid and vibrant, precisely because you are no longer grasping or avoiding it, and thus no longer trying to dull or dilute it. You no longer turn the volume down. You might every cry harder, laugh louder, jump higher. Choiceless awareness doesn't mean you cease to feel; it means you feel fully, feel deeply, feel to infinity itself, and laugh and cry and love until it hurts. Life jumps right off the screen, and you are one with all of it, because you don't recoil."[9]

Ken Wilber

"In fact all the sheaths from gross to subtle are not that One who experiences ...Among all these sheaths and states through which the individual goes, there is only one element

which is not involved – the Observer, the Atman, which is eternal. One should rise and go beyond the sheaths."

The Shankaracharya.

It is not outer awareness,
It is not inner awareness,
Nor is it a suspension of awareness.
It is not knowing
It is not unknowing,
Nor is it knowingness itself.
It can neither be seen nor understood,
It cannot be given boundaries.
It is ineffable and beyond thought.
It is indefinable.
It is known only through becoming it.

Isha Upanishad

This we have now
is not imagination.

This is not
grief or joy.

Not a judging state,
or an elation,
or sadness.

Those come
and go.

This is the presence
that doesn't.

Rumi

Part Ten

STILLNESS AND MANIFESTATION

Purusha and Prakriti

In the Advaita Tradition, the Universal Consciousness is described as having two aspects known as Purusha and Prakriti. Purusha is the still unmanifest Consciousness that is without change while Prakriti is the manifest nature of that Consciousness. It is the whole phenomenal universe that is subject to movement and change, birth and death, growth and decay.

PURUSHA **PRAKRITI**

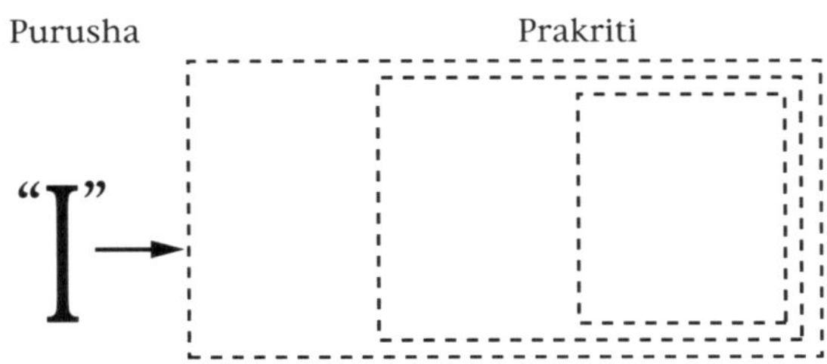

In life, with all its demands, it is very easy to become caught up with the drama taking place on the line of time and forget the still, formless, unmanifest Consciousness. In our lives, it is necessary to give importance to both these aspects of Consciousness. We need to play our parts in life, as best we can, with as much enjoyment and enthusiasm as possible and also give attention to the great stillness that underlies the world of manifestation.

There are times when the curtain of life parts and the world loses its importance for us as the sole reality. At such times we become aware of the still Source. It is as if we have been totally absorbed by the images on the screen and suddenly we turn around and notice the projector. This process often happens as a result of life's difficulties, such as illness, bereavement, relationship break-ups or redundancy. We begin to wonder if there might be something more than we are experiencing in our daily lives. We wonder if there is another aspect to life and ourselves that we are overlooking in some way.

When this is first noticed, a great change often starts to take place in our outlook. We begin to reassess what it is that we really regard as important. At this point we may also start to notice all sorts of coincidences, as if we are being lovingly lead along a new path whose existence we never suspected. When this happens life takes on a very different quality. Those things that had previously appeared as difficulties or obstacles are now seen as reminders and stepping stones. Life is no longer a separate hostile affair but rather it is perceived as infinitely benign and all its many phases are seen as signposts leading us back to the unmanifest Source.

Maya

The word "Maya" is usually translated as "illusion" and refers to our being caught up solely with the manifest world of time and change, and seeing it as a separate reality.

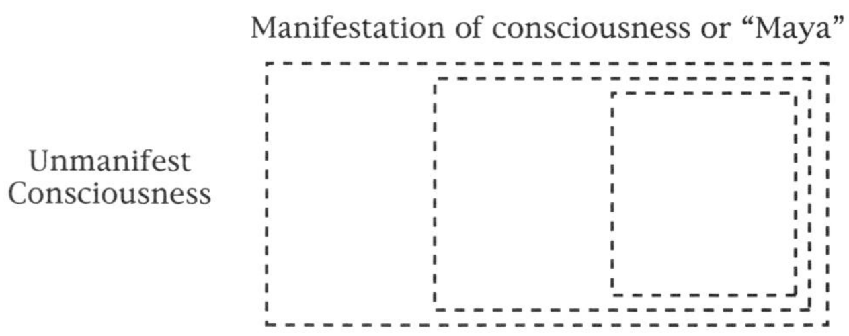

There are many versions of a story in Indian mythology that tell of a man in a forest clearing asking a holy man the meaning of the word "Maya". But very soon he finds himself becoming caught up in life and forgetting all about the question. He marries, has children and is involved in many dramas. Eventually, after a whole lifetime, he dies and suddenly finds himself back in the forest clearing with his question about Maya still hanging in the air. A whole lifetime has passed and yet it is as if no time had passed at all.

But Maya is another name for Prakriti and refers to the nature of the unmanifest Consciousness or Purusha.

We experience it as "illusion" when we forget that it is all the manifestation of the One Consciousness and consider it a separate reality having its own independent existence.

Once we acknowledge that everything is Consciousness then the world of Maya is no longer experienced as an illusion or as a separate reality, but is seen as it truly is, as the "nature" of Consciousness.

The drama

One of the ways that the concept of stillness and manifestation is made more practical is through the understanding of life as a drama or play.

From the Non-dual perspective we are all aspects of the One Consciousness playing roles in an unfolding drama. We are not separate but all different facets of the same Being.

Each person has a unique role, and it is in following our own inner light and where it leads that we gradually discover what that role is. And it does not have to be anything dramatic, just being ourselves is enough.

When we feel that we are just the actors in a drama, then we can play our roles with detachment. We are able to take the necessary action in the moment as the situation demands and then let go of it. This way we can play our parts without the feeling of being a separate independent doer, but rather as aspects of one whole, responding to an unfolding drama. This attitude brings with it a feeling of great release and freedom.

When we perceive ourselves to be separate doers, then we become like the actor who forgets that he is an actor, and takes his part as real, and in doing this we take upon ourselves an immense but imagined burden.

The Benedictine monk and writer, Bede Griffiths, likened death to the moment when the lights go up at the end of a film. We had been totally engrossed in the film but then, suddenly, we remember who we really are but had forgotten - "Yes, of course, this is who I am".

When we live life with an awareness of who we really are, beyond the level of the drama, then life's sudden changes do not come as such a shock. And while we are living life to the full, we are also preparing for the ultimate moment of "letting go", the death of the physical body.

Quotations

"We have known the word Sat, that which is. Whatever is has the existence, and that is the substance, but this substance is of two types. One is the immobile existence and the other is mobile existence. The immobile and mobile existences are known as Purusha and Prakriti, i.e. the Absolute and the Creation. If one experiences any sort of movement or any sort of sensation, or any sort of intake, one is still in the world of Prakriti. Meditation is the process to take one from movement to non-movement (stability). As long as there is any appreciation of sound or smell, then one is still separated from the immobile substance. That substance is there and in true meditation one becomes that substance."
The Shankaracharya

"We should see Param-Atman in everything. If we do that, we receive special favours from Him. Then this curtain of ignorance lifts up and the Maya, which has been cheating us all the time, no longer does so and begins to help us instead." *The Shankaracharya*

"Either you can accept it as blissful or miserable, it depends on how you place yourself in relation to this drama. If you are attached to the drama, if you think it is real, then the general picture is of misery. If you are detached, if you think it is a drama, and there is a part of be played by you, then it is all blissful." *The Shankaracharya*

"The Creator created the universe in all its different aspects and forms. He observes the drama which He has created. All who take part in this play and know its mystery and essence are detached. They play their part and enjoy it.

Those who do not know its mystery become identified with their parts and are bound by them. When they lose their identification they too can enjoy playing their part in the grand drama without being bound.

There was a man from the country who visited his city relatives. To entertain him the relatives took him to the cinema. They bought expensive tickets for the back row, but their country cousin was insulted at being put at the back and insisted that they sit at the very front. All went well until suddenly a lion appeared on the screen and looked as if it would jump out at the audience. Our friend took his stick and struck at the lion to defend himself. The screen was broken, the film stopped, and the place thrown into darkness and confusion. At first no one could understand what had happened, then they realised that in the audience was a man who had never been to a cinema before and took the film to be real. The same applies to those ignorant people who regard what goes on in the world as the whole reality and become identified and involved, leading to foolish actions; when the real significance of the grand drama is known, these people can play their part with detachment and enjoyment." *The Shankaracharya.*

"As this mirror-mind awareness (or constant consciousness) grows stronger, the gross waking state becomes more and more "dreamlike," in the sense that it loses its power to overwhelm you, to shake you, to make you believe that passing sensations are the only reality. Life starts to look like one great big movie, and you are the unmoved Witness watching the show. Happiness arises, you witness it; joy arises, you witness it; pain arises, you witness it; sorrow arises, you witness it. In all cases, you are the Witness, and not some passing surface wave of silly sound and fury. At the centre of the cyclone, you are safe. A deep and inward peace begins to haunt you; you can no longer manufacture turmoil with quite the same conviction.

But that doesn't mean that you can't feel desire, hurt, pain, joy, happiness, suffering, or sorrow. You can still feel all of those; they just don't convince you. Again, it's like being at the movies. Sometimes you get so caught up on what is happening on screen that you forget it's just a movie. At a thriller, you might actually become frightened; at a romance, you might start crying. Then your friend leans over and says, Hey, lighten up, it's just a movie, it's not real! And you snap out of it.

Enlightenment is ... to snap out of the movie of life. To wake up, to shake it off. You are, and always have been, at the movies, as the Witness. But when you take life seriously - when you think the movie is real - you forget you are the pure and free Witness and you identify with the little self - the ego - as if you were part of the movie you are actually watching. You identify with somebody on screen. And therefore you get frightened, and therefore you cry, and therefore you suffer altogether.

With meditation, you begin to relax in your seat and just watch the movie of life, without judging it, avoiding it, grasping it, pushing it, or pulling it. You merely Witness it: you employ the mirror-mind, you rest in simple, clear, spontaneous, effortless, ever-present consciousness."[9]

Ken Wilber

"If you don't realise the source,
you stumble in confusion and sorrow.
When you realise where you come from,
you naturally become tolerant,
disinterested, amused,
kindhearted as a grandmother,
dignified as a king.
Immersed in the wonder of the Tao,
you can deal with whatever life brings you,
and when death comes, you are ready."[17]

Tao Te Ching

Part Eleven

OBSTACLES

It is sometimes helpful to become aware of the obstacles that block our experience of the light of Consciousness and see why we view the world and ourselves as other than they are - as small and separate rather than as a unity.

We saw in our study of the Antahkarana how the play of the gunas, and our individual samskaras, affect the transparency or opacity of the Antahkarana and its ability to reflect and be a vehicle for the light of the Universal. We saw how it is important not to identify with these changing states but rather, to witness them from a point of stillness.

The Advaita Tradition describes three further obstacles that relate to the hearing and assimilation of knowledge. These are called Mala, Vikshepa and Kashaya.

Mala literally means, "dirt" and refers to an opaque covering of the Antahkarana so that new ideas are unable to enter and be assimilated. It is related to the passive guna, Tamas, and is a result of past tendencies or samskaras.

Vikshepa is distraction or dispersion and is related to the active guna, Rajas. The mind is unable to settle down to listen to what is being said, and instead darts around following different trains of thought.

The remedy prescribed for these two obstacles is meditation since it both stills the mind and removes the opacity allowing the light of Consciousness to shine through.

The third obstacle, Kashaya, is a word used to described the sticky resin or gum that comes from a tree. It refers to identification with particular ideas or ways of thinking. When this happens we are unable to appreciate or understand the new knowledge being presented due to our association with past ideas.

One of the methods recommended for the assimilation of new ideas is "manana" or "chewing". We study a particular idea for sometime and the often, at an unexpected moment, its meaning becomes clear. Sometimes a whole sequence of ideas are illuminated and become rich with meaning.

Often it is enough just to notice the existence of a particular obstacle. Once we notice something, we are already separate from it, we are already the witness of experience and no longer the experience itself. It has lost its power to overwhelm.

When we do just observe the obstacles and no longer struggle with them, they often start to change their character, and rather than being obstacles they become reminders of what we have forgotten.

Quotations

"Antahkarana is made to stand still by the process of meditation and the greater the stillness which is achieved the greater is the force of the Universal - the oneness with the Universal is being experienced.

But this is only half the answer, because there are two things - Mala and Vikshepa - while Antahkarana is just like a pool of water. If the water is not still, Antahkarana is not still - then the reflection will be poor. At the same time if there is mud, if it is dirty - then too, even if it is still, then the reflection will be poor. So the meditation helps to do both things, it removes the mobility or the rippling of the water - it removes Vikshepa - as well as cleansing, which means the removal of the Mala." *The Shankaracharya*

"About the three types of coverings which we have - because of these coverings communication is hampered and is not possible between the disciple and the Teacher. One of them is usually predominant in each individual. The first one is Mala (literally translated as "dirt") the opaque dirt which prevents all penetration into the Antahkarana of the individual, so that he doesn't understand anything of what is being preached, or the way being shown to him. The second is the Vikshepa (distraction) which is when the discourse is taking place and someone is giving the teaching, the attention of the individual goes somewhere else just after catching the first sentence, so he cannot listen to what is being

said. And the third one is Kashaya (veil) which is the sort of covering out of which there is practically no impression gained by the individual, and this Kashaya is due to sticking to certain ideas which have been taken without any reason - (sort of blind belief). These are the three ways due to which communication of pure reasoning is not possible. One has to get rid of these before reason can prevail."

The Shankaracharya

"If people have regularly come to hear the good words and yet have not found the point of rest, the main reason is the nature of their ingrained tendencies. They still have a certain disturbed element in them and it prevents them making their own all that is told to them and, when they go back, they again get engulfed in their previous tendencies. They should continue to meditate and reflect again and again about what they have heard so that in due course their previous tendencies will be removed and there will be room for taking in new things they have been told.

To illustrate this:

There were two ants: one was living on a mountain of salt, the other was living on a mountain of sugar candy. It happened once that the two ants met and they talked about themselves. The ant who was living on the sugar candy was given a piece of salt by the other ant. When she tasted it, she said, 'It is horrible! How can they live on this?' The first ant invited the other to her home and so the second ant when to the sugar candy mountain with all her sisters and other ants. Thinking there wouldn't be enough for them to eat there, they all took a small piece of salt into their mouths. When they arrived, the sugar candy ant gave them a small piece of candy, but since they already had a small piece of salt in their mouths, the two tastes got mixed up - and they said, 'You praise your own home so much, it is almost the same as ours'. Then the first ant said, 'Well, go and wash your mouths and then come again.' They did so and again tasted the candy and found that it was really sweet. So then they never went back to their own home."

The Shankaracharya

"One of the fundamental characteristics of man's attitude to himself and to all his surroundings is his constant identification (attachment) with what pleases or displeases him. The word identification means that you lose your own identity and become hypnotized by other things instead. The equivalent Sanskrit word is more revealing. It is kashaya, the word for sticky resin or gum from a tree. Insects are attracted by its aromatic odour and get stuck in it. Psychologically it means that the mind gets stuck in anything that attracts it; and the universal thing that everybody's mind gets stuck in is one's ego. It's a waste of time making a list of things one can be identified with. What is important is to get to hate this feeling - the nasty sticky feeling of being identified and losing one's freedom of choice.

All our lives should be lived as if we were playing a role in a drama, for only then will we be free of the bondage and the danger of disaster brought about by being captivated by one's false ego. This is the way to overcome identification."

Dr Roles

"Be content with what you have;
rejoice in the way things are.
When you realise there is nothing lacking,
the whole world belongs to you."[17]

Tao Te Ching

The Guest House

"This being human is a guest house
Every morning a new arrival.
A joy, a depression, a meanness,
Some momentary awareness comes
as an unexpected visitor.
Welcome and entertain them all!
Even if they're a crowd of sorrows
who violently sweep your house
empty of its furniture,
still, treat each guest honourably.

He may be cleaning you out for some new delight.
The dark thought, the shame, the malice,
and invite them in.
Be grateful for whoever comes,
because each has been sent as a guide from beyond."

Rumi

"We see that each time we let go of the hindrances we recondition the experience of their next appearance. Every time we let go of the hindrances, we increase our capacity for letting go perhaps an instant sooner the next time around. We see with an increasing easiness of mind that each time doubt or fear or resistance mechanically arise they are received in an expanding awareness which has little tendency to implode in identification and intensify suffering. Then even the hindrances are seen just as process passing through; then anger reminds us to love, fear reminds us to soften, and such as restlessness and boredom do not agitate the mind, but act as a focus for the deep calm of a steady awareness. So much that had been thought of for so long as enemies in the mind becomes reminders, allies, of the heart. The hindrances are no longer obstacles but instead become stepping stones across the river of forgetfulness."[10]

Stephen Levine

Part Twelve

SHRADDHA

The concept of "shraddha" is one of the most profound and reassuring aspects of the non dual teaching and can have a big impact on the way we view our lives.

The word "shraddha" is sometimes translated as "faith". But it is not the sort of faith that is the result of blind belief. Rather, it is the faith in the Universal that comes as a result of knowledge gained from direct experience.

For example, we are sure that the sun will rise in the morning and set in the evening because it has always done so on previous days. This is not a vague hope but a certainty in our minds, based on past experience.

So shraddha is the sort of faith in the Universal that contains no doubts. It is also a certainty based on past experience. Often, when we look at events in our lives in isolation, they can appear pointless. But, sometimes when we get a glimpse of a larger perspective, we can see the events as a necessary part of a larger whole. We may have gained some understanding or insight from a particular experience that later plays an important part in our life's drama. A single incident or meeting can often show the purpose of and give meaning to a whole series of previously misunderstood events.

When we observe this, then it can give us a deep faith in the process of life's unfolding, a deep trust in the author of this plan and a feeling that He does seem to know what He is up to after all.

Then, when we are confronted with a situation that we do not understand, we are able to remember our past experience and trust that it does have a purpose and that we are still being looked after and led through life. For why should the Universal suddenly forget us if we have been looked after up until now?

This can give a very different attitude to our lives. The need to manipulate events and people changes to a sense of responding appropriately to the needs of the moment, of allowing and watching the drama of life unfold, and playing our individual roles without a sense of being a separate "doer" of our actions or creator of events.

So it seems that shraddha is not something we can create, but rather it is gained from the observation of life and from the realisation that we, and all creation, are part of the manifestation of Param Atman.

Quotations

"Suppose there is a man for whom we have great respect. The more we become acquainted with him the greater will be our love and respect, and as this process continues your love for him goes on increasing. Your love does not diminish in increasing acquaintance. In this case the man is the Atman. To know something about the Atman is necessary because, unless we become acquainted with the properties of the Atman, love cannot exist. When the acquaintance becomes full then there is satisfaction. Certain knowledge about the properties of Atman, such as how Atman behaves, is necessary for the development of love. For this the Sanskrit word "shraddha" is necessary - shraddha is a form of respect *The Shankaracharya*

"The Param Atman alone is unchanging; it always remains the same. But this Param Atman is also manifesting through all these different forms, which we directly encounter and derive knowledge through them. It is quite possible, therefore, that our concept of Param Atman would keep on changing as the Knowledge, and the level of the individual would, changing all the time. One does wonder (since one's concept is changing), what really is happening. In fact, there is nothing wrong in all this; one's concepts must keep on evolving, and the Knowledge and concept of Param Atman will continue to become subtler and subtler; but within this ever-changing concept about this unchanging Absolute, there is one thing which never needs to be changed - that is the faith in Param Atman. If one has the faith - complete unchanging faith then one should not worry

about the changing concepts." *The Shankaracharya*
"If once during our life-time an unshakeable faith in Param Atman is established, that is, that we belong to the Param Atman and Param Atman belongs to us - then we are out of reach of all harm." *The Shankaracharya*

"GOD has created me to do Him some definite service; He has committed some work to me which He has not committed to another. I have my mission - I may never know it in this life, but I shall be told it in the next.

I am a link in a chain, a bond of connection between persons. He has not created me for naught. I shall do good, I shall do his work.

I shall be an angel of peace, a preacher of truth in my own place while not intending it - if I do but keep His commandments.

Therefore I will trust Him. Whatever, wherever I am, I can never be thrown away. If I am in sickness, my sickness may serve Him; in perplexity, my perplexity may serve Him; if I am in sorrow, my sorrow may serve Him. He does nothing in vain. He knows what He is about. He may take away my friends, He may throw me among strangers. He may make me feel desolate, make my spirits sink, hide my future from me - still He knows what he is about."

Cardinal Newman

"You have to let life be before you will be able to let life go."[11] *Stephen Levine*

Part Thirteen

PRACTICE

Within the non dual traditions there are many different ways prescribed to help practise the teaching in our daily lives.

In the Advaita Tradition the very idea of practice can sometimes appear as a paradox and can give us the feeling that the Self is something to be achieved in time, rather than being ever present and available in the 'Now'.

But at the level of the drama of life, it is often some sort of systematic practice that brings our minds to the realisation that the Self is ever present and available now. And it is important to remember that the very act of practice is one of the ways that the Self is unfolding itSelf in the drama of creation. So that practice, rather than being a process to gain an objective in the future, is seen as an expression of the Self at this moment.

In the Shankaracharya's system the purpose of many of the methods is to give the individual an abundance of the sattvic energy of being, so that the Antahkarana loses its opacity and the inner and outer worlds are experienced as a single unity.

Any new practice can usually take a little time to become established, but if we persist, new ways of thinking and being gradually become second nature and part of our lives.

In addition to meditation we have already looked at several different approaches. Early in 1973 at a public talk the Shankaracharya spoke of a series of seven steps that could be practised on a daily basis. They are presented here in the form that the Shankaracharya first gave them, followed by a version with comments by Dr Roles.

Quotations

"There are seven stages like the steps of a ladder, each leading to the next, till the final stage is reached.

1. *The first stage is good actions, which lead to -*
2. *The second stage, which is good thoughts.*
3. *Good thoughts lead to the third stage, which is decrease in bad thoughts.*
4. *Decrease in bad thoughts leads to the fourth stage, which is predominance of Sattva.*
5. *Sattva leads to the fifth stage, which is decrease in worldly attractions.*
6. *Decrease in worldly attractions leads to the sixth stage, which is giving up of worldly objectives.*
7. *Giving up worldly objectives leads to the seventh and final stage, which is freedom from all thoughts about one's own self and one's personal profit."*

The Shankaracharya

"Seven Steps of a Practical Way to the Supreme Self

1. ***Good actions:*** *with attention, "worthy of the supreme Self."*

2. ***Good thoughts:*** *benevolence, cheerful attitude, good will.*

3. ***Decrease of bad thoughts:*** *ill will, criticism, grumbling.*

4. ***Sattva begins to dominate:*** *change of values, waking up of warmth.*

5. ***Decrease in power over us of worldly attractions:*** *less identification.*

6. ***Giving up worldly objectives*** *(i.e. ambitions, dropping out of the rat race, but observing one's duties and obligations).*

7. ***Liberation from all thoughts about oneself*** *and one's profit and loss.*

"It must be remembered that these are not rigid steps, that their characteristics are all potentially present in each of us,

for isn't the Atman Himself (Real I) present in us, though not realised by us owing to the cloud of ignorance that surrounds Him. Consequently each day we probably have experiences for moments of at least six of these steps, our task being to make them more and more permanent in us. I have to start each day with he first step, and often several times in the day, but I try never to stay on that first step for long!" *Dr Roles*

"Sattva is described mostly as light - a light which is steady. So one of the major manifestations of the presence of Sattva is this illumination of any type of work one takes on. If one finds oneself afraid to tackle a new situation or one has doubts on certain types of subject, that instantly means lack of Sattva.

What can one do to change the situation so that there is abundance of Sattva in one's being? The collection of certain good qualities is essential. The good qualities are these:

1. *One should always love to speak the truth: so there is no disparity between what one thinks and what one says, or between what one says and what one does. There should be complete correspondence of ideas with activities.*
2. *Cultivate the love of people, encouraging them in turn to express their love through certain types of activity.*
3. *Be magnanimous in dealing with those around you."*

The Shankaracharya

"Every time I recognise or acknowledge the ever-present Witness, I have broken the Great Search and undone the separate-self. And that is the ultimate, secret, non dual practice, the practice of no-practice, the practice of simple acknowledgement, the practice of remembrance and recognition, founded timelessly and eternally on the fact that there is only Spirit, a Spirit that is not hard to find but impossible to avoid."[9] *Ken Wilber*

"We've talked so much! Remember
what we haven't said.

And keep working. Exert yourself
toward the pull of God.

Laziness and disdain are not devotions.
Your efforts will bring a result.

You'll watch the wings of divine attraction
lift from the nest and come toward you!

As dawn lightens, blow out the candle.
Dawn is in your eyes now."

Rumi

Part Fourteen

LIBERATION

Dr Roles' main message to us at the end of his life was the need to go "all out for liberation", via the simple system of Non Duality. We should not be satisfied just with the study of the mechanism but each person should find the truth inside and for him or herself.

What does this mean? We are all very different and we find that different approaches work for us at different stages of our lives. We seem to be naturally attracted to that aspect of the teaching that is most important for us at a particular time.

Throughout this framework we have looked at the key points in the Advaita Teaching and we have tried to see how they can have practical application for our daily lives.

Perhaps the central point of the teaching is the nature of our essential divinity and the illusion of our separation. The fact that we already are that which we are seeking and yet do not see it. And, in not seeing it, we go on looking, unaware that we already are it.

So liberation is not about gaining anything new, but about giving up the misidentification of our sense of self with body or mind and acknowledging our true identity. Ignorance is simply this mistaken identity.

The various methods such as meditation, self-enquiry and bhakti are ways of helping the mind give up this unreal identification.

It is important that we do not see our individual roles in life as separate from this realisation. For each of our lives, just as it is, expresses the Universal. In a strange way our "not knowing" is an aspect of the Reality and a part of its manifestation. Without the ignorance there would not be the gradual "return to source", and the whole unfolding drama of creation. As Bede Griffiths put it: "Ignorance is a stage of knowledge."

It was this realisation that led the Buddhist sage Nargarjuna to state, "Samsara and Nirvana are one"* So, as Dr Roles suggested, all that is required is a change of attitude, of acknowledging what already is.

* Samsara is the manifest world of time and change while Nirvana is liberation.

Karma

The doctrine of karma is usually regarded as the law of cause and effect. It is often associated with the idea of the repetition of lives; our actions and desires in one life lay down a blue print for possible future lives.

The concept of karma is also often perceived to be a form of retribution whereby we are punished or rewarded for our deeds in a past life. The limitation of this view is that it implies that we are all separate independent entities rather than aspects of one whole. I feel that a more accurate and compassionate understanding of karma is that it is the process of experience by which we are led to see through the veil of illusion so that we can become aware of the underlying Reality and the nature of our true Selves.

In the different religious traditions different concepts are used to illustrate this process. In Buddhism and Hinduism, for example, there is the concept of reincarnation whereas in Christianity there is the idea of purgatory. Both of these concepts can be seen as metaphors which indicate that we may need more experience before we are able to see through the veil of illusion and perceive Reality as it is. In this sense karma is not something generated by our past misdeeds but is our particular life path whereby we are led out of illusion and back to an understanding of the reality of who we already are.

In the Advaita Tradition the way to escape from the law of karma is not just by creating better causes or paying off debts but by realising deep in our being that there never was a separate entity to accumulate karma or debts in the first place, and so acknowledging the One Consciousness of which we are all part.

So karma is seen to be a purely relative concept that depends for its existence on the illusory notion of our being separate entities. In this way the Advaita Tradition offers us a very direct path to liberation. It advises us to go direct to the Source of Consciousness by acknowledging our true identity and seeing the Universal as the real Doer and not being content to settle for lesser levels of identity. It is then rather like the concept in Zen of the "Gateless-gate". We may strive all our lives to get through a gate but once through it, we look back and wonder whether there really was a gate and whether there was really anybody to go through it.

Meaning

Although our true Selves are beyond definition and categorisation, at the level of our daily lives meaning is very important. The psychiatrist and Auschwitz survivor Viktor Frankl suggests that there are three main ways by which we can arrive at meaning in our lives. The first is by creating some work, or by doing something and the second is by experiencing something or someone so that "experience" becomes as valuable as "achievement". This opens up the avenue to meaning for those who, due to their circumstances, may be incapable of physical achievement. The third way, he suggests, which is open to anybody no matter how difficult their situation in life, is the ability to transform or grow beyond oneself.

The process of life, with its varied situations and experiences, can gradually evoke and bring out different aspects of our characters that we may not have been aware of previously. In the same way the varied aspects of life, if seen from a different point of view, can lead us back in the causal chain of identity so that life itself becomes our means of transformation. Its not that we are becoming anything new but rather that life's process can cause our more finite levels of identity to fall away. It is quite a common experience to see someone go through a difficult life situation and emerge more soft, gentle and compassionate as a result. It is as if a layer of identity has been dissolved and what lies underneath begins to shine through. In this way life's journey can take us back through identifying only with the physical body to an awareness of the subtle and the causal realms, to the great stillness that lies behind experience and phenomena. This is our true nature and the nature of the whole Universe.

Quotations

> *"It is not far away. It is right within our reach. It is only because we don't believe it, do we? We have been so trained and brought up and taught that we are sinful beings and cut off from God since Adam and Eve in the Garden, we just don't believe any of it."* — *Dr Roles*

"We very foolishly complicate things. We do everything the wrong way round. One begins to realise that everything has already been provided by Param Atman. One has only to be what one is." *Dr Roles*

"Time is part of the material world. Where there is space, there is time. A long journey takes much time, a short journey less, but in the spiritual world time and space have no validity. One can't think of time in relation to self-realisation. The Self which is to be realised is here, there and everywhere. No-one has to journey to find it. It is found only in Oneself." *The Shankaracharya*

"Atman knows Atman. There is no other agency to know the Atman because there is none, but as long as our ignorance is there, the illusion will be there. This would see Atman as something to be known. In fact Atman only knows the Atman." *The Shankaracharya*

"Realisation of the Self can be gained in this very life. In fact, Self-realisation is not something which is to be gained afresh. We are already the Self; the Self alone is. It is ignorance that makes us imagine that we have not realised the Self. When this ignorance is removed through Self-knowledge, we realise our eternal Self-nature."

T.M.P. Mahadevan

"Yes. We keep on teaching the Creator His business, whereas if you will allow the Creator to do the creating, things happen, and that's what means keeping Param Atman in your heart ... loving the Param Atman and keeping Him in your mind and heart and letting Him get on with it for you. And this comes from stillness, and if you first of all still the ordinary noisy psychology which is going on in one's mind all the time, you get the stillness on the Subtle level where Nature provides moments in between desires and the thought processes come to an end. Then if you can just take it a step further, and when you snap our of all those psychological processes which are silly little habits, and when you are lucky

enough to feel complete satisfaction with what is, then you get the peace on the Causal level, and it amounts to total surrender to and complete faith in the Will of the Absolute. You will find that you accept what comes without reflection or opposition. This is really what giving up means. Giving up your own feelings that you are the doer, your own ambition, your own opinions, and allowing Nature to do it." *Dr Roles*

"The universe also unfolds itself in two ways; one way is the way of ignorance (Avidya) in which we imagine ourselves to be the 'doers' of actions and are, therefore, subject to the law of Karma, i.e. 'as you sow, so you reap'. The other way is like the performance of a drama, in which the actor, acting as a thief or a saint, knows he is <u>*not*</u> *a thief or a saint. For him, therefore, the law of Karma does not hold. For example, in cases where the Param Atman took the part of a man, according to Hindu scriptures, he was not really a man. Thus he was not bound by the Karmas he did as such. This cannot be the case with a person who identifies himself with his actions. If anyone thinks that he has won a victory today, the law of Karma lays down that he would suffer a defeat tomorrow."* *The Shankaracharya*

"All experiences of happiness or misery, fear or delusion are of the individual spirit. As long as there is this unreal identification man is bound by his deeds and subject to birth and death. All this bondage is caused by ignorance. With true knowledge comes freedom. The way to this knowledge is to devote oneself to the worship of God and to see Him in all."
Srimad Bhagavatam

"If you are not the body and do not have the idea 'I am the doer', the consequences of your good or bad actions will not affect you. Why do you say about the actions the body performs 'I do this' or 'I did that'? As long as you identify yourself with the body like that you are affected by the consequences of the actions, that is to say, while you identify with the body you accumulate good and bad Karma."[12]
Ramana Maharshi

"A Brahmin may play various parts in a drama; yet the thought that he is a Brahmin does not leave his mind. Similarly, when one is engaged in various empirical acts there should be the firm conviction "I am the Self", without allowing the false idea "I am the body, etc." to rise. If the mind should stray away from its state, then immediately one should enquire, "Oh! Oh! We are not the body etc.! Who are we?" and thus one should reinstate the mind in that (pure) state. The enquiry "Who am I?" is the principal means to the removal of all misery and the attainment of the supreme bliss. When in this manner the mind becomes quiescent in its own state, Self-experience arises of its own accord, without any hindrance. Thereafter sensory pleasure and pains will not affect the mind. All (phenomena) will appear, then, without attachment, like a dream."[13]

Ramana Maharshi

"It doesn't matter how lonely you are; it doesn't matter how bad the situation is, or how hopeless the outlook; it's just that lesser values have to be broken down until one finds this thing in all our hearts which is God and Love and Truth and one's Self all at the same time. When you touch it, it's very familiar; there have been thousands of ways in which it has been said and acted and lived. *Dr Roles*

"To those who have realised the nature of Reality, there is nothing old or new, and conceptions of shallowness and depth are meaningless. Those who speak of it do not attempt to explain it, establish no sects and open no doors or windows. That which is before you is it. Begin to reason about it and you will at once fall into error. Only when you have understood this will you perceive your oneness with the original Buddha-nature." *P'ei Hsiu*

"All doubts disappear after the realisation of God. Then the devotee meets the favourable wind. He becomes free from worry. He is like the boatman who, when the favourable wind blows, unfurls the sail, holds the rudder lightly and enjoys a smoke." *Gospel of Sri Ramakrishna*

Part Fifteen

NOT THE DOER

One of the most practical concepts that derives from the non-dual model is the idea of not being the "Doer". We have seen that the very word "Advaita" or non-duality means "not two" and implies that there is just One Consciousness that is everything. We saw in the study of Ahamkara and the Antahkarana that when this is applied to our sense of personal identity it is possible to equate our sense of Self with less than who we really are. In other words, we tend to identify with the vehicle rather than with Consciousness itself.

When seen from the point of view of the whole drama of creation, this mistaken identity is not an accident for it is this that gives rise to the creation drama of apparently separate entities all interacting with each other.

Sometimes, when we look back at our lives from a greater vantage point, it is possible to see a pattern as if we are led through life with events unfolding in a way that we, as separate entities, could never have planned or foreseen. As we observe this more and more it begins to undermine our sense of being a separate "doer" and gradually gives rise to a feeling of watching a film or a play unfolding. With this understanding comes a lessening of the need to manipulate life and other people and, at the same time, there is an increase in a deepening feeling of "Self Consciousness", an awareness of our true identity or sense of "I AM" which is beyond body and psyche.

From this perspective our lives and the lives of others are all perceived as the unfolding of the One Consciousness. One of the advantages of this viewpoint is a lessening in the feelings of guilt and regret for past actions, a lessening of fear about the future and an increase in understanding and compassion for the apparent faults and actions of others.

For some the idea of our sense of self being Universal can appear frightening. Then it is important to remember that all that is really lost is the moving mind's identity with an imagined past or future and an opening up to our true identity that responds to each event as it unfolds in the present.

One of the most effective ways of dissolving the feeling of separation is to ask the question, "Who am I?" Through this process, lesser levels of identity are dropped and the mind returns to its source. Thoughts are then seen to arise out of this unmanifest source and dissolve back into it. Artistic inspiration and dreams arise in this way and are not something that we generate separately. By perceiving these thoughts and feelings as arising from a separate self we perpetuate the illusion of being a separate doer. We are then like the ants in Rumi's story of a pen writing on a piece of paper. In the story the first ant attributed the writing to the pen and said, "How wonderful it is that the pen can do this writing." Another ant said, "No, it is not the pen but the hand that holds it." Another said, "No, it is the arm that gives movement." Thus the ants went back in the causal chain until a wise ant said, "No, the writing is caused by the Universal Spirit that gives movement to all things. " So the illusion of separation and of being a separate doer is caused by not going far enough back in the causal chain until we arrive at the ultimate cause which is Universal and without cause.

When this is perceived as part of our own experience the consensus view we have of our separate self generating its own actions begins to dissolve and we become aware of our true identity that is without boundary.

So with this realisation, how do we live our lives? Probably just as we do now. We try to use our talents and gifts to play our own role in the drama of life. This may include being passionate about both those things that delight us and also those things that we deplore, taking the necessary action in the moment and giving up the results to the Universal. But also, somewhere at the back of our minds, is the realisation that we, as separate entities, are doing none of it.

Quotations

"All claims of being the doer of actions or enjoyer of objects relate to ego. When wisdom dawns, then the distinction between the witness and the doer becomes clear and one

understands that one is the witness and not the doer or enjoyer. This witness is the stillness; the claims of doing and enjoying are the din of the market, the realm of movement, the place of businessmen. In the Gita Lord Krishna says, 'The fool, whose mind is deluded by egoism, considers himself to be the doer.'

As long as there is the feeling of doing and achieving, the individual is in the movement and not in stillness.

If one hangs a coat in the wardrobe, the inanimate coat can't put itself on anyone's body. It will remain where it is. When you put it on, it goes with you everywhere. So it is with the body. The body is the coat; if you claim the body as your own, then it accompanies you everywhere, but as soon as you stop claiming, then it takes its proper place as part of nature. Then the 'I' becomes the witness, having no attachment." *The Shankaracharya*

"The Mundaka Upanishad says, 'There are two birds, two dear friends, who have made their home on the self-same tree. The one pecks at the sweet fruit, while the other looks on in silence, not eating.

The first is the human spirit, who feels sad and bound by ignorance. But on beholding the power and glory of the universal, be becomes free from sorrow'.

They co-exist as they sit on the tree of creation and one of them enjoys the fruit of the tree. These two sweet friends are the Absolute and the individual. The individual is involved with the creation and its fruits. It feels as if it is seeing, eating, sensing and enjoying the world, and, in doing so, gets attached to the world, whereas the Absolute, although it is in and with the creation is in no way involved with the creation and only watches and enjoys.

We do not see or understand that the changes take place in our nature and not in the Atman. Atman is not subject to change. One who understands this becomes very light and walks in freedom and without carrying the load of the world. He is one who enjoys the drama in its true sense and never associates himself with the characters of the drama. Our job is simply to watch and enjoy." *The Shankaracharya*

"The only thing required of the individual is a gradual, but fundamental change of attitude to oneself and one's life. Instead of saying, 'I am doing, I am succeeding, or I am failing,' (with all the turmoil and frustration that such an attitude sets up), we must learn to say: 'The Param Atman is doing it all. Please keep me at my own job and stop my personal psychology from interfering with Your purpose.' Then you'll have time and energy to use your talents for your own role in the big drama." Dr Roles

"One of the fundamental characteristics of worldly life is the illusion of being the independent doer – of having free will. It is very difficult to maintain that individuals are the doers of anything, for the whole creation is a manifestation of the Absolute who is the real doer. He has made His whole show in such a beautiful pattern that keeps changing from one moment to another, and must also keep on multiplying. The whole thing is going on by virtue of the creative impulse given by the Absolute; He is the independent one, He is the free one, and He is the real doer.

Part of the show is our human nature with its capacities of memory and thinking. If one takes the load of the 'past' and the 'future' upon oneself, the journey becomes hard and treacherous; 'past' and 'future' appear terribly big, and it is very difficult to walk along the path if one carries this load. 'If I had done such and such', one thinks, 'then this or that could have been achieved'; or, 'if I hadn't acted as I did, all this trouble could have been avoided'. One should always keep oneself light-hearted and free of this burden.

In fact, the load is on the mind, the physical body has nothing to do with it; but because the mind governs the physical body, the physical body also suffers.

One of the best analogies is the shadow play of puppets. There is someone holding the strings and moving them, but they appear to be moving themselves and to be the real doers.

The whole of creation is very much like a puppet show, with the strings being held by somebody else.

Take the example of a cinema show, where the film is being shown on the screen and the people keep on looking at these moving pictures. On the screen you see mountains, buildings, seas, and fights, love scenes and religious scenes. All types of scene are being enacted on this screen. Some people watching are like the puppets, and they get animated by the scenes. One should be able to see the things which are happening in the world but only as a silent observer. See all the pleasures on the screen, but don't get involved and moved off course." *The Shankaracharya*

"On the mast of a ship a bird was sitting quietly while the ship left the port and was going out to sea. The bird was confident that it could fly the distance back and reach its own place. After a long time with the ship far out to sea, it was evening, and the bird was thinking that its children would be crying for it at home, and it tried to fly home across the ocean. But it could not find the shore, so thought it must have mistaken the direction and returned to the mast for a rest. When it was rested it set off again in another direction, but the same thing happened – it could not find the shore because the distance was too great. It went to the South, to the North, to the East and West, but in the end it realised there was nothing it could do, so it returned to the mast and once more sat quietly.

Now it was confident again, but in another way – not that 'I can do', but 'I must go where the mast of the ship is taking me.'

So long as you are in the individual ego and not on the universal level, you will be thinking that you can do it yourself." *Dandi Swami*

"A man will reckon some things to be well done and others to be evil, but our Lord does not see them so...For as all natural things have been made by God, so all that has been done is in some way God's doing. It is not difficult to see that the best deed has been done well, and as the best and highest deed has been done, so the least deed has been done just as well. All this is in accordance with the nature and

plan that God has decided for everything from before creation. There is no doer but he.

I saw with absolute certainty that he never changes his purpose in anything whatever, and never will. Through his ordering, everything has been know to him from the first. It was all set in order before a thing was made, and so it was ever to remain. Nothing shall fail of his purpose. He made all things in abundant goodness, and therefore the trinity is for ever satisfied with what he has done.

He showed me all this to my great happiness, as if he were saying, "Look, I am God, I am in all. I do everything! I never cease upholding my work, and I never will. I am guiding everything toward the end I ordained for it from the first, by the same might, wisdom and love with which I made it. How can anything be wrong?" [14]

Mother Julian of Norwich

"So long as the feeling 'I am doing' is there, one must experience the result of one's acts, whether they are good or bad. How is it possible to wipe out one act with another? When the feeling that 'I am doing' is lost, nothing affects a man. Unless one realises the Self, the feeling 'I am doing' will never vanish." *Ramana Maharshi*

"The Creator created the universe in all its different aspects and forms. He observes the drama which he has created. All who take part in this play and know its mystery and essence are detached. They play their part and enjoy it. Those who do not know its mystery become identified with their parts and are bound by them. When they lose their identification they too can enjoy playing their part in the grand drama without being bound.

A man from the country was visiting his relatives in the city. To entertain him, they took him to the cinema. They bought expensive seats in the back row, but their country cousin was insulted at being put at the back. He insisted that they sit in the very front. All went well until suddenly a lion appeared on the screen, and looked as if it would jump at the audience. The visitor took his stick and struck at the lion to defend himself. The screen was broken, the film stopped and the place was thrown into darkness and confusion. At first no one could understand what had happened; then they realised that in the audience was a man who had never been to a cinema before and took the film to be real.

The same applies to those ignorant people who regard what goes on in the world as real and become identified and involved, leading to foolish actions; when the real significance of the grand drama is known, these people can play their part with detachment and enjoyment."

The Shankaracharya

"Looking at things is the great magic formula on our road to self-realisation. Simply looking alters the quality of that which is looked at because it brings light – consciousness – into the darkness. We are generally so keen to alter things that we find it difficult to grasp that all that is required of us is the ability to look. The highest human goal – whether we call it 'wisdom' or 'enlightenment' – consists in being able to look at everything and to realise that it is perfectly fine just as it is. This is what is meant by true self-knowledge. So long as there is anything that still disturbs us, so long as there is anything that we feel needs changing, we have simply not attained self-knowledge."[15]

Thorwald Dethlefsen and Rudiger Dahlke

"Accept the world as it is.
If you accept the world
the Tao will be luminous inside you."[17]

Tao Te Ching

"Practice not-doing and everything will fall into place."[17]

Tao Te Ching

"To become only the observer and allow everything to happen as it has to happen." *The Shankaracharya*

Part Sixteen

THE WITNESS

We have seen how much of the non-dual teaching is concerned with realising our identity as the still impartial Witness or Observer. How can we understand this further and make it more practical?

One of the most fundamental mistakes we make is perceiving 'being the witness' as something we have to do or as a special state to be achieved. We seem to imagine we have to divide ourselves in two in some way. The Shankaracharya often uses the analogy of a cinema show or a drama to illustrate what is meant by 'the witness'. From this point of view it is as if we are all just watching a well-written play unfold with happy scenes, tragic scenes, love scenes and so on. When we identify our sense of self with just the mind/body mechanism we feel that we are one of the characters we are watching in the film. We suffer or are happy according to the scene being acted out and we forget that we are not actually that character but just a watcher of the show. In feeling ourselves to be the character in the film we are then constantly trying to change what is being shown, like the story of the man from the country who jumped out of his seat to hit the lion on the screen.

So how does this change? In the chapter on 'Not Being the Doer' we saw that if we observe the unfolding of our lives very closely we begin to notice that it is rather like a well-written film that is unfolding often despite our interventions rather than because of them. With this realisation we begin to relax and cease to try to manipulate life so much when it does not appear to be going the way we think it should.

When we do relax we begin to give up our sole identification with the mind/body mechanism and we start to notice that our identity is already and always has been the Observer or Witness at the causal level. Nothing has changed but we have relaxed and noticed that we already are the great stillness that just quietly observes its own play.

Our attitude then goes through a considerable change. Instead of wondering what we should do next it becomes more a question of wondering what will happen next. Its not that we cease to act and just stay in bed all day; there is an awareness of whose show it really is and who is doing it all and that we are ultimately that. This state is often likened to a mirror that simply reflects all that it sees without comment or judgement.

In our journey through life we are gradually led to this realisation. If our identity remains at the level of the drama we are subject to the 'slings and arrows of outrageous fortune'. When life goes the way we think it should we will be happy and when it does not we will be unhappy. In this way we are led to look for that which is beyond change. As Rumi put it in the Divani Shamzi Tabriz:

> "How pleasant are the pains he makes you suffer while gently he draws thee unto HimSelf."

As the Witness is the ultimate observer, it cannot itself be observed. Anything that can be observed is subject to change and that which changes will also be subject to suffering. Realising our identity as the Witness and living in the present moment is a way of going beyond suffering which is always available to every person no matter what their circumstances.

Quotations

> *"With the idea of enjoying the whole creation with an impartial attitude, one might ask where is the sense of being good, what is good and bad? The question never gets resolved. In fact there is neither good nor bad - it is simply our labelling. It is our preference for one or the other which makes one good and the other bad – our impertinence which makes one good and the other bad.*
>
> *If one could keep to this state of silent impartial observer, one would see that none of these things exist. One stays in the present, and one acts as the occasion demands and the whole thing passes. Wise men once discussed this question of driving happiness out of all the multifarious aspects of the*

world, and the discussion led to the conclusion that one should not enable oneself with either side (physical or subtle), but should simply observe; because the Absolute is in everything, and this creation is a most efficient mechanical organism which is functioning according to the laws of the Absolute, so one should always see the Absolute behind all these passing phases.

Once Swami Rama Tirtha, who was from the Punjab, saw a black adder in his path; it was a puff adder with its hood open. He just smiled and laughed and said, "Oh my God, you have come before me in such a frightening shape – but forgive me, I don't like your shape this time so please go away.' And the puff adder went away.

This shows how to behave as an unprejudiced and silent observer who has no duality (no mental division into 'good' and 'evil')". *The Shankaracharya*

"Everything is made of the Absolute – the causal, subtle and physical. When one sees the physical manifestations in movements, one forgets that the physical never moves by itself unless the subtle initiates it, so all movements of the physical body are manifestations of the subtle behind them. Control of unnecessary movement is useful, but no amount of force will produce any good result, for inevitably this will create a chain of opposing reactions. In response to such force, one turns to negative ways of not doing this or that, which results only in further chaos.

Just as the physical is governed by the subtle, so is the subtle by the 'causal'. Let this 'causal' come into the picture. The causal does nothing, but only witnesses; just let him witness and the process will change. No need to impose rigid controls nor need one be anti-movements. The presence of the observer is quite enough to undo unnecessary movements. The physical body is very mechanical, so for some time the movements will prevail even if the observer is there, but observer works on the purity of subtle body and when that is achieved all unnecessary things will fall away. In the control of the physical body, rigid and forceful formulas are not useful. If physical body moves, then in fact men-

tal movement is responsible. Only allow the observer to watch, and the rest will be done." *The Shankaracharya*

"One should identify oneself with the universe itself. Everything that is less than the universe is subjected to suffering." *Simone Weil*

"Thus the ways of Param-Atman are beyond human comprehension. Many things are happening around us – some good, some bad – and we are unable to explain them. We wonder how Param-Atman, who is good, could cause or allow bad things to happen. But 'good' and 'bad' are just comparative notions, and there cannot be anything good unless there is something bad by contrast.

These notions of 'good' and 'bad' constantly create conflicts in our minds and do not allow us any peace. The way to get over all this is to dissociate ourselves from the events viewed and associate ourselves with the viewer of the events – the Param-Atman.

Param-Atman is the cause of everything and is everything. The world we see is nothing; it was never anything in the past and will never be anything in the future. Param-Atman is, and is everything; he is the friend as well as the enemy; he is the saint and the householder; he is the beast and the man; he is the sorrow, the attachment and everything else.

Such things worry us as they do in a dream; yet nothing of the dream remains when we wake up. What else could all this be except the most wonderful show?

> *Once Vidyasagar (a well-known author and reformer) was watching a theatrical performance in Calcutta, which showed in a very realistic manner the terrible atrocities directed by the rulers on their subjects. The show was so realistic that the reformer stood up and hurled a shoe at the stage. This created confusion in the hall. The organizer appeared on the stage and said: "This shoe is the greatest possible tribute to our skill".*

If a man-made show could be so effective, what can we say to a show staged by Param-Atman? But even while causing all this, Param-Atman does nothing at all. Understanding this sheds all the burden from the mind, just as waking up removes all the tensions of a fearsome dream. Actually for pacifying a troubled mind nothing could be more refreshing than to regard everything as part of a show staged by Param-Atman. Weep if you must, and laugh if you can, but that underlying thought should be there.

The past is never exactly the same again. Stop worrying about it; keep cheerful, for cheerfulness is your real shape. The clothes you are wearing must wear out; the smoothness of your skin must go; wrinkles must appear on your face; your body must lapse into the coils of time. Take all that in your stride and play the part assigned to you."

The Shankaracharya

"Man is not a creator, he is a reflector, a witness, an image and likeness of that which is – the only activity there is – the infinite Mind unfolding itself to itself perpetually in the most glorious, harmonious set of completely specified and detailed forms."

Glen Shaeffer

"Thus, as I right now rest in this simple, ever-present Witness, I am face to face with Spirit. I am with God today, and always, in this simple, ever-present, witnessing state. Eckhart said that "God is closer to me than I am to myself," because both God and I are one in the ever-present Witness, which is the nature of intrinsic Spirit itself, which is exactly what I am in the state of my I AMNESS. When I am not an object, I am God. (And every I in the entire Kosmos can say that truthfully).

I am not entering this state of ever-present Witness, which is Spirit itself. I cannot enter this state, precisely because it is ever-present. I cannot start Witnessing; I can only notice that this simple Witnessing is already occurring. This state never has a beginning in time precisely because it is indeed ever-present. You can neither run from it nor toward it; you are it, always. This is exactly why Buddhas have never entered this state, and sentient beings have never left it.

When I rest in the simple, clear, ever-present Witness, I am resting in the great Unborn, I am resting in intrinsic Spirit, I am resting in primordial Emptiness, I am resting in infinite Freedom. I cannot be seen, I have no qualities at all. I am not this, I am not that. I am not an object. I am neither light nor dark; neither large nor small; neither here nor there; I have no color, no location, no space and no time; I am an utter Emptiness, another word for infinite Freedom, unbounded to infinity. I am the opening or clearing in which the entire manifest world arises right now, but I do not arise in it – it arises in me, in this vast Emptiness and Freedom that I am"[5]

"When I rest in the pure and simple Witness, I notice that this awareness is not an experience. It is awareness of experiences, it is not itself an experience. Experiences come and go. They have a beginning in time, they stay a bit, and they pass. But they all arise in the simple opening or clearing that is the vast expanse of what I am. The clouds float by in this vast expanse, and thoughts float by in this vast expanse, and experiences float by in this vast expanse. They all come, and they all go. But the vast expanse itself, this Free and Empty Seer, this spacious opening or clearing in which all things arise, does not itself come and go, or even move at all.

Thus, when I rest in the pure and simple Witness, I am no longer caught up in the search for experiences, whether of the flesh or of the mind or of the spirit. Experiences – whether high or low, sacred or profane, joyous or nightmarish – simply come and go like endless waves on the ocean of what I am. As I rest in the pure and simple Witness, I am no longer moved to follow the bliss and the torture of experiential displays. Experiences float across my Original Face like clouds floating across the clear autumn sky, and there is room in me for all."[5]

"As I drop all objects – I am not this, not that – and I rest in the pure and simple Witness, all objects arise easily in my visual field, all objects arise in the space of the Witness. I am simply an opening or clearing in which all things arise.

I notice that all things arise in me, arise in this opening or clearing that I am ..The clouds are floating by in this vast opening that I am. The sun is shining in this vast opening that I am. The sky exists in this vast opening that I am; the sky is in me. I can taste the sky, it's closer to me than my own skin. The clouds are on the inside of me; I am seeing them from within. When all things arise in me, I am simply all things. The universe is One Taste, and I am That."[5]

Ken Wilber

"The perfect person employs the mind as a mirror. It grasps nothing; it refuses nothing; it receives, but does not keep."

Chuang Tzu

"The Master observes the world but trusts his inner vision. He allows things to come and go. His heart is open as the sky."[17] *Tao Te Ching*

"Ignorance," Patanjali reminds us, "is the identification of the Seer with the instruments of seeing." Instead of Witnessing the body, we identify with it. Instead of Witnessing the ego, we identify with it. Instead of Witnessing suffering, we identify with it. And yet inevitably we are controlled by that with which we identify; we are tortured by all that we have not transcended. Thus lashing ourselves to the masts of misery, we suffer the outrages of space and time and terror." [9] *Ken Wilber.*

"An old man said to the Zen master, Dai-soko: 'I don't know, I've been at this work for forty years and I seem to be going backwards. I can only conclude I am both dim and dull'. Master Dai-soko replied: 'There is indeed dimness and dullness but that which perceives dimness and dullness is neither dim nor dull, reside in that.'" *Zen Story*

Part Seventeen

PRASAD

Most of the concepts used in the Advaita tradition are metaphors that help us give up our identification with lesser levels of Reality. They are pointers to the truth rather than the truth itself which is totally expressionless and beyond rational formulation. These concepts can help dissolve our feeling of being a small separate self, acting on an external world and relating to other separate selves. One such concept is the idea of 'prasad'. This word is usually translated as being a 'gift' so that whatever circumstances we find ourselves in can be regarded as a gift from the Universal Consciousness.

This is not always an easy concept to accept since many of the circumstances we find ourselves in appear far from 'gift-like'. Yet this can be a very effective way of turning around the view we usually have of events and learning not to judge phenomena from too narrow a viewpoint.

We have seen how events in life that can appear unpleasant at the time, having no apparent purpose, can be seen later as significant parts of a consistent plot. It is sometimes necessary to reverse the view we have of what is really beneficial to us and hence see what is really a gift.

If the main purpose of our lives is the realisation of our true nature then the things that help us in this process may be different from those things which, for instance, only make us materially wealthy. Difficult events and crises can often help our consciousness give up its sole identification with form and start to turn inwards to find its source.

The varied events in our lives are now seen from a very different perspective. The American doctor and writer, Andrew Weil, suggested that negative paranoia is the mirror image of mystical experience. Paranoid people see the world as being a conspiracy against them while mystics see the world as a conspiracy arranged on their behalf. Consequently, from the non-dual perspective, nothing is perceived as accidental. Every event that occurs is seen as coming from the Universal to help us discover the greatest gift of all, our true nature.

When we regard all experience as a gift there is a lessening of feelings of blame, both of self and others. When we apportion blame we move into a world of separation and we miss the point of the experience and of the drama.

So regarding every event as a gift or 'prasad' from the Universal Consciousness is a way of learning to shift the view we have of phenomena from a limited ego perspective to that of our true Selves.

Quotations

The basic meaning of initiation is to connect the individual with the universal (Param-Atman). The mantra given enables one to establish a connection with the Lord. After initiation, whatever one eats, one should think of it as a gift. After initiation, whatever we do, we do it with surrender to the Almighty; whatever we receive for our own use we should regard it as 'Prasad' – a gift from the Almighty. We must carry the idea that we own nothing. Everything has now become God's; we are using everything with His permission, and not as owners. This helps with the elimination of the individual ego – then the pure realisation of the Self develops." *The Shankaracharya*

"Whatever we have is part and parcel of the cosmos. This body represents the earth of the cosmos; mind represents moon, the power of seeing represents the sun, etc. So that whatever we have, the individual is a particle of the cosmos. Normally 'Prasad' is associated with what we offer to the Lord and then receive back. It is the gift from the Lord but, before we get the gift, we make our offering. The best way, connected with devotion, is to regard whatever we have as a present from the Lord. In whatever circumstances we have been paced – that is also the Prasad of the Lord.

For instance – we cook our food; then, if we offer it first to the Lord and take it as a gift, that will be very healthy. It will be very helpful for spiritual progress if we accept every-

thing only after first offering it. It is so even in doing our work, performing our duties. Supposing we are in the profession of law – when we start our day's work we first offer it to Him. 'With your help, God, with your Prasad I'm going to argue this case.'

So, whatever we do, we should first offer it and make it a Prasad. This purifies your mind and your body, and you become more suitable – eligible for God's spiritual roles."

The Shankaracharya

"(Now) I will talk to you of matters indifferent. Hark, O Sufi, open your spiritual ear very wide.

Whatever blow may come to you from Heaven, always be expecting (to receive) a gift of honour after it;

For He is not the king to slap you and then not give you a crown and a throne on which to recline.

The whole world has (but) the value of a gnat's wing; (but) for one slap there is an infinite reward.

Nimbly slip your neck out of this golden collar, (which is) the world, and take the slaps (that come) from God.

Since the prophets suffered those blows on the nape, in consequence of that affliction they have lifted their heads (high).

But (always) be present (attentive and ready) in yourself, O youth, in order that He may find you at home.

Else He will take back His gift of honour, saying, 'I found nobody in the house.'"[3] *Rumi*

"I don't see what we have deserved. I do find people complain an enormous amount. I cannot see why so many people think things should be better than they are. I don't see where their idea of what is better, what is ideal, comes from. It seems to me we get more than we deserve. If one is in any sort of good state ....the pleasures of creation, of society, of sensation surround us and are there to be enjoyed. There is a glory and a mystery and excitement all round us, which many people who complain a lot, refuse to look at, refuse to accept, refuse to take in. It's all there like a great box of sweets, and they say, 'No, these aren't the sweets we wanted."[16]

P.J. Kavanagh

"I came to realise that everything that is part of life is inevitable to it and must therefore be good. I could not be bounced high upon the crest of ecstasy and joy unless I also knew the dreadful depths of the trough of the great waves of life. We are born to die. If death were not, life would not be either. Pain and weakness and evil as well as strength and passion and health are part of a beautiful pattern of life. And as I grew up, I learned that life is richer and fuller and finer the more you can understand not only in your brain and intellect, but in your very being, that you must accept it all without bitterness the agony, without complacency the joy. Dimly I perceived that it was because I was I that life came to me like this."[18] *Helen Thomas*

"You've got to say yes to this miracle of life as it is, not on the condition that it follows your rules. Otherwise, you'll never get through to the metaphysical dimension."[1]

Joseph Campbell

"When one brings to one's knowledge the different aspects of the glory of the Absolute, then one feels grateful for the bounty which is being provided for the individual, and immediately the hard heart melts." The Shankaracharya

Part Eighteen

ACTION IN THE WORLD

In the study of Advaita the question is often asked, "How does the practice of this teaching affect the way we act in the world and in our daily lives?"

Apart from the principles of Sanatana Dharma the teaching provides little guidance in the way of codes of behaviour. Perhaps this is because, as our identity gradually shifts from limited to Universal, so too does the way we act. It was Albert Einstein who once said that the most important question we can ask ourselves is: "Is the Universe a friendly place?" It is this fundamental belief that determines how we respond to life.

When we perceive ourselves as separate entities acting on an external mechanistic outside world, such a view can give rise to a need to manipulate the world and other people for our own ends. It can be a model of the survival of the fittest. The world can be perceived as a frightening place, where anything could happen at any moment if we put a foot wrong – and if we don't someone else will.

With the realisation that we are all aspects of one whole comes a change in the way we react to the world and those around us. Individuals are now seen as all aspects of the One Consciousness playing different roles in an unfolding drama. So when we act, we act to the best of our understanding at that moment, according to our nature, situation, health and available energy and then surrender the results to the Universal. Because it is Consciousness that acts, events will often unfold in a way we never expected. As Joseph Campbell put it: "Doors will open where you didn't know they were going to be".

Perhaps this approach could be summed up by the injunction from the Gospels, "Do unto others as you would be done by". With the realisation that there are no 'others' but only different aspects of the One Self, the need of the ego to manipulate its surroundings lessens.

The motivating factor then changes from one of personal gain to Universal compassion, both for one's fellow human beings and for the world at large. This means that from the perspective of the non-dual world we can take the appropriate action in the moment, let go of the results and trust that "Thy will be done".

Quotations

"1 Physically, be everybody's servant – devote yourself to universal service.

2 Emotionally, give importance to the Supreme Being, always remembering His never-ceasing good will and benevolence.

3 Intellectually, identify yourself as One with Param-Atman who witnesses everything impartially and reveals Himself in all that you perceive."

The Shankaracharya

"When you have some sort of love, the effect is that you bring enthusiasm into the work to keep it continuous. To bring about this situation, if we think and try to impress upon ourselves that all the work which we are undertaking for any result is only in the service of the Absolute, so that we offer as our service whatever we do, then the individualistic approach or the egoistic approach would not intervene in the work.

That is the true way and one should see that one serves the Absolute, and does not think to achieve things personally by one's own deeds." *The Shankaracharya*

"When the idea that Atman alone is truth and the rest is Maya or illusion has been fully appreciated, then one will experience expansion of light, power, knowledge and service, and accordingly the limited ideas of individuality and relationships will break their barriers and go on extending in proportion to the depth at which this idea is rooted in the being. The being will be full of enthusiasm and one will be

naturally able to know more, teach more and be of service to many more people than before. The world would become a family. The limited would become unlimited, small would become large, and darkness be transformed into light. Love would prevail everywhere. The individual would love all and all others would love the individual."

The Shankaracharya

"Since the causal realm cannot be described, one learns about it from its effects. One can see it in the activities and dispositions of those who provide themselves with spiritual rest. There are three prominent features.

First, they show love and affection towards everything they encounter. All activities are initiated with love, and then held and nourished with love till they come to their fulfilment. All relationships with individuals or activities, direct or indirect, are illuminated and guided only by love and affection.

Second, their ideas, intentions or motives are pure and simple. Purity and simplicity widen the horizon, and they think and work for the whole of humanity and only through the laws of the Absolute. The divisions of groups, races or nations disappear and only natural laws are employed. Their thoughts naturally encompass the whole of the human family, and its intrinsic goodness.

Third, the physical movements of such people are tuned to the natural rhythm, and the result is simplicity and economy of movement. They never rush into any situation, are never agitated, and perform all actions in an efficient, sublime and refined way. Whatever they do will emerge from stillness, be held in stillness, and again submerge in the same stillness which they experience in this great total immobility. This is an idea or a standard for the common man to aspire to, if he somehow awakes to the need to improve his state."

The Shankaracharya

"One should take it as a sort of drama, and only play one's part without any attachment to any of the activities which one takes. Once you have established yourself in a state in

which you simply act as you can, then just as in the dramatic performance the actor enjoys acting, and the onlooker enjoys the play." *The Shankaracharya*

"In everything, everywhere, we see Param-Atman. The feeling you have for your family grows to include your community, then your nation, and then the whole world; from being limited we become unlimited and the whole world becomes our family, and we have the feeling 'everything is mine and I belong to everybody'." *The Shankaracharya*

"The root of suffering is man's ego-hood, which separates him from his fellow-beings and from the sources of reality. How can he overcome his suffering? Basically, there can only be two answers. One is to overcome separateness and to find unity by regression to the state of unity which existed before awareness ever arose, that is, before man was born. The other answer is to be fully born, to develop one's awareness, one's reason, one's capacity to love, to such a point that one transcends one's own egocentric involvement and arrives at a new harmony, at a new oneness with the world."[19] *Lama Anagarika Govinda*

Part Nineteen

FOUR WAYS

In the Indian tradition there are generally considered to be three main routes to Self Realisation. These are: karma yoga or the way of action, bhakti yoga or the way of devotion and jnana yoga or the way of knowledge. People follow one or another of these routes according to their temperament or disposition.

Through karma yoga devotees serve the Universal through service to others and action in the world. It is not uncommon to meet people who seem to have an inner light as a result of the work they do. Often this can be seen in the caring professions such as nursing or teaching or even in the deliveryman at the local shop. Through service to others the separate ego is transcended in favour of the Universal.

Bhakti, or the yoga of devotion, is a more emotional way where our lives are dedicated to the service of the Universal. No special conditions are necessary. We continue to live our lives but we are no longer acting just for personal gain but as a way of glorifying the supreme Self. Action is taken in the moment, whether it is sweeping or washing up or any other activity, and the results are surrendered and given over to the Universal. This again is a very profound yoga since it can be practised whatever our circumstances, by the commuter going to work, the busy mother with children or the ill person in bed. Through love and devotion the separate ego is dissolved as we perceive that the part of us that loves is also the object of our love and our sense of duality ceases.

Jnana yoga is the way of knowledge. This does not mean that to follow this way you have to study astrophysics or do differential calculus. It is simply the process of using the capacity for reason and the discriminative mind to discover its own source. We are often led to ask ourselves such questions as "Who am I?", "What is the nature of mind?", "Where do my thoughts come from?" and so on. By this process of reasoning, which is sometimes called 'self-enquiry', the mind gradually gives up lesser levels of identity until it returns to its unmanifest source, which is Universal and experienced as total stillness. Here also, as with karma and bhakti yoga, the sense of a separate identity is transcended.

We have already seen how the way of the householder is sometimes known as the 'Fourth Way' and is for people who, by temperament, are not predisposed to just one of the traditional ways. However, the methods of the different traditional ways may be followed depending on our needs and circumstances at different times in our lives. Sometimes we will transcend our separate selves through the way of action while at other times we may work through love and devotion and at other times the emphasis is on the use of discriminative reason.

The way of the householder is also called the 'Way of Understanding' since discipline is not imposed from outside but it is up to each individual to listen to their own inner voice to find what is the right approach for them at a given moment. When we do this we discover that each one of us is being led along our own path of realisation in a way which is unique for ourselves. Living our lives then becomes something which is not separate but our own route to realisation. Events that previously had appeared accidental now become significant parts of this unfolding. It is in observing this that we are again led from the apparent separate self to the source of Consciousness in realising who it is that lives.

Quotations:

The following six quotations are all from the Shankaracharya:

> *"You don't have to prepare a very long scheme for practising devotion. Whatever you are doing, you can continue to do the same thing; you have only to change your approach. If you are doing anything with a view to some personal gain, then the approach should be: 'I am doing this not for any gain, but as a service to God. What I am eating, I am not eating just for my own satisfaction, but as an offering - it has been given to me by the Lord to enable me to serve Him.' So that whatever you do, you connect it with the Lord – that will become devotion – you don't have to change your course of action;*

the action will be the same, but the object will be different."
"Dedication to the service of the Param-Atman and to other people in thoughts and actions, at all times and in all circumstances is the way to stabilise your mind in your own great Self.

When the idea that Atman alone is truth and the rest is Maya or illusion has been fully appreciated, then one will experience expansion of light, power, knowledge and service, and accordingly the limited ideas of individuality and relationships will break their barriers and go on extending in proportion to the depth at which this idea is rooted in the being. The being will be full of enthusiasm and one will be naturally able to know more, teach more and be of service to many more people than before. The world would become a family. The limited would become unlimited, small would become large, and darkness be transformed into light. Love would prevail everywhere. The individual would love all and all others would love the individual."

"Love and knowledge are the same thing but the function of love is to join together and that of knowledge to tell, to illuminate.

In love, knowledge is helpful. For strengthening knowledge, love is essential. In the absence of love, knowledge would not be powerful enough to influence people. Knowledge only helps us to decide what is right and wrong, but it cannot alter things; love can alter them.

Without love, knowledge is incomplete and without knowledge love is incomplete because, in the absence of knowledge, love would go away. If there is knowledge, then love would be maintained. As love increases, knowledge also goes on increasing. Without knowledge, love is not expansive; and without love, knowledge is not allowed to play its full part."

"In love you always give and don't demand in return. By giving, you allow things to happen.

When people love someone, they forget that real love means no demands from the beloved.

The Absolute, or the Atman, wants the human heart in its simplicity and directness. When that has been dedicated, everything will follow in the course of time, and one need not worry whether man's actions are small or big, good or bad, efficient or inefficient. That doesn't matter - the real dedication He requires is only of the heart."

"Knowledge is unlimited and available at all times. It manifests itself according to the need of the time. It is only available when the need arises. The stream of love and truth is one, but man catches it in two different ways, by heart or by mind. By heart he means his love, by mind he means his knowledge. But in fact the stream of love and truth is always the same. It is always present in the world and always will be present in the world but people will only take as much as their destiny offers or as they need.

Knowledge is not bound to any land or place. No place is favoured. Knowledge is everywhere, all over. If certain types of people are prepared at a place, they will receive it. Preparation of mind is the only key to where this knowledge will descend. If people at a particular place take to the ordinary way of life, they will get ordinary knowledge. If at a certain place people are preparing themselves for higher knowledge, certainly it will be available. No place is particular for knowledge. Anywhere, anytime, anybody who is looking for this knowledge must get it, because the Absolute is not for a single race, colour, creed or nation."

"Travelling is as refreshing for some
as staying at home is for others.

Solitude in a mountain place
fills with companionship
for this one,
and dead weariness
for that one.
This person loves
being in charge of the workings

of a community.
This one loves
the ways that heated iron can be shaped
with a hammer.
Each has been given
a strong desire for certain work.

A <u>love</u> for those motions,
and all motion is love.

The way sticks and pieces of dead grass and leaves
shift about in the wind
and with the directions of rain and puddle-water
on the ground, those motions
are all a following
of the love they've been given."

Rumi

"Don't look for bits of grain like an ant.
Look for the granary master,
and you'll have grain and the Presence
as well."

Rumi

"How wondrously supernatural,
And how miraculous this!
I draw water, and I carry fuel!"

P'ang-yun

Part Twenty

TOP DOWN

The non-dual model is a model of reality in which practically everything is totally different from the way it appears to our limited sensory apparatus. Almost every event and situation in life can be turned around and seen from a totally different perspective from the one we normally use.

One way to look at phenomena is from below. From this viewpoint everything is perceived as separate and divided; man and the world, man and God, good and evil, life and death etc. The physical world is seen as the main reality with consciousness as a remote spark contained deep within our brains, the product of millions of years of evolution. From this viewpoint the realisation of our true identity is seen as a remote and far away objective, obtainable only after years and lifetimes of hard struggle and effort.

In Advaita, the viewpoint is from above. From this perspective all separation vanishes and everything is seen as an aspect of one undivided whole. Consciousness is not contained within matter. Rather, matter is seen as a ripple on the surface of Consciousness, as its manifestation, and not as something separate. Nor is Consciousness seen as a remote far away objective any more since it is what we already are, right now. All that is required is a change in our perception. This only appears difficult because we tend to disbelieve it and may need convincing. It is also important to understand that these different ways of viewing phenomena are only different levels of perception. The Reality is from the top down; everything is the manifestation of Consciousness. The bottom up view is just a trick of light which can be discarded once Reality is perceived at first hand.

When we look from above and see everything as part of one whole, many of the aspects of life that we find incomprehensible when viewed from below, disappear. For example, we are often surprised by the number of coincidences that happen in life and the examples of synchronicity. We may think to ourselves, "fancy that working out the way it did or that person turning up just when they were needed." When looked at from the 'above' view this should not be a surprise as it is not a question of separate individuals interacting with each other but rather aspects of the One Mind interacting with itSelf. When events do not unfold in the way we had hoped or intended this enables us to trust the process of life's unfolding and see that it is all part of a greater design which we are unable to comprehend from a limited perspective.

In this way people are no longer seen as separate but all aspects of One Universal being. The One Consciousness looks out through all of our eyes to see and appreciate its own manifestation in the world around. When we see the mist on a river in autumn or the sunset over a distant range of hills in midsummer or the smell of new mown grass in springtime or any other sense perception, it is Consciousness perceiving itSelf. As that acknowledgement takes place the separate self vanishes leaving only Universality.

So Consciousness is no longer a remote far away objective, obtainable only after lifetimes of struggle. Nor is it something that will only be experienced when we are in a better state or life is arranged in a way that is more agreeable to us. Rather it is something that is impossible to avoid, ever present in every aspect of life that we encounter.

Quotations

"We have had everything upside down and back to front".
Dr Roles

"We have, I think, a much quicker and more direct way to look at it, from above. Going from below one can turn off into side alleys at so many points. It requires such a long and patient determination and constant help to keep on the right road. Now we have the opportunity of learning how to look at it from above." *Dr Roles*

"The point as regards ourselves is that in relation to Consciousness we need to keep the broad picture and not go into detail too much". *Dr Roles*

"All is consciousness, there is no proof to anyone, to any individual, that there is anything else but consciousness. To assume that there is anything beyond consciousness is pure hypothesis. But we deviate from it the whole time. We keep on insisting that there is something outside consciousness that is beyond it, the image of the visual world. We have hypothesised a thing called matter, with its forces which give rise to the image, forgetting that the image is primary and is consciousness. But we now worship something that is purely hypothetical, and is secondary, but we are taking it as primary. Therefore what we arrive at has to be upside down...." *Glen Shaeffer*

"What is God? God is Absolute, unrestrained, existing being. To talk about God is impossible; even to call God the Absolute is to give a boundary where there is none, because Absolute being is a concept of the mind and binding.

Fire enlightens or burns, and water you can drink or be drowned by. These two qualities cannot be separated from fire and water. As these qualities are a requisite of these two materials, so is God for creation. He is obliged to show Himself. The manifestation is a way of knowing Himself. He created the universe to see Himself – to see His own reflection as in a mirror, and to know Himself. This first manifestation is knowledge and love. Nothing exists except God, so that we and everything are part of God. This universe is nothing, but the appearance, or manifestation, of the Absolute being." *Resuhi Baykara*

"This All is one universally comprehensive living being, encircling all the living beings within it, and having a soul, one soul which extends to all its members; every separate thing is an integral part of this All by belonging to the total material fabric, while, in so far as it has participation in the All-Soul, it possesses spiritual membership as well. Each several things is affected none the less by all else in virtue of the common participation in the All!" *Plotinus*

"We are living in a world that is absolutely transparent and God is shining through it all the time. This is not just a fable or a nice story. It is true. If we abandon ourselves to God and forget ourselves, we see it sometimes, and we see it maybe frequently. God manifests Himself everywhere, in everything – in people and in things and in nature and in events." *Thomas Merton*

"All the Buddhas and all sentient beings are nothing but the One Mind, beside which nothing exists. This Mind, which is without beginning, is unborn and indestructible. It is not green nor yellow, and has neither form nor appearance. It does not belong to the categories of things which exist or do not exist, nor can it be thought of in terms of new or old. It is neither long nor short, big nor small, for it transcends all limits, measures, names, traces and comparisons. It is that which you see before you – begin to reason about it and you at once fall into error. It is like the boundless void which cannot be fathomed or measured. The One Mind alone is the Buddha, and there is no distinction between the Buddha and sentient things, but that sentient beings are attached to forms and so seek externally for Buddha-hood. By their very seeking they lose it, for that is using the Buddha to seek for the Buddha and using mind to grasp Mind. Even though they do their utmost for a full aeon, they will not be able to attain it. They do not know that, if they put a stop to conceptual thought and forget their anxiety, the Buddha will appear before them for this Mind is the Buddha and the Buddha is all living beings. It is not the less for being manifested in ordinary beings, nor is it greater for being manifested in the Buddhas."[20] *Huang Po*

"Heraclitus said that for God all things are good and right and just, but for man some things are right and others are not. When you are a man, you are in the field of time and decisions. One of the problems of life is to live with the realisation of both terms, to say, 'I know the centre, and I know that good and evil are simply temporal aberrations and that, in God's view, there is no difference.'"[1] *Joseph Campbell*

"Religion, whether it be Christianity, Buddhims, Hinduism, Theosophy, or any other kind of 'ism' or 'sophy' or system, can only take us to the one point where all religions meet and no further. That one point where all religions meet is the realisation – in no mystical sense, and the more worldly and everyday and practical the better – of that fact that God is everything, and everything is God." *Arthur Osborne*

"If you thoroughly accept the coherence of the omnipotent goodness of a God that is love and life as well as truth, if you thoroughly accept that, you have to reject as completely unreal and nothing, any suggestion of its opposite. When one has immersed oneself, even for a second in such a coherent view, not in a misty way, but in a calculational way almost in a logos manner, and you have accepted the coherence and the unity and the goodness and the love of One Universal Consciousness, Self-reflecting with you as its witness, then you will discover that you have no problem any more. It works every time as long as you can get into that, even for a second, because it has eliminated the other suggestions which looked absolutely real.

There is only one source, and that source must be entirely good because if it had any opposites built into it, it would not be eternal. We all believe this is an eternal thing and to have existed eternally already and forever, because it means it has not one iota of opposite built into it. Any such thought is a pure belief or suggestion which can be erased completely by immersing into such a coherent picture, a picture which fills out more and more as it is turned to more and more. Because it is infinite and ever-present, we don't turn to it very often and so we grow very slowly. But the whole of it is available this minute, right now! Now is eternal life.

That's my view and it works in practice when applied. That's my experience."

Professor Glen Shaeffer - Talk at Colet House

"The Tao that can be told is not the eternal Tao
The name that can be named is not the eternal Name
The unnamable is the eternally real
Naming is the origin of all particular things
Free from desire, you realise the mystery
Caught in desire, you see only the manifestations
Yet mystery and manifestations arise from the same source
This source is called darkness
Darkness within darkness
The gateway to all understanding."[17]

Tao te Ching

Part Twenty One

VIVEKA

One of the key concepts in the non-dual traditions is that of 'Viveka', as the function of discrimination is known in Advaita. This is concerned not so much with deciding what we should or should not do in our daily lives, but more with the process of using the discriminative faculty to see beyond the world of appearances. This means seeing beyond the surface display of phenomena on the line of time, beyond the pairs of opposites to the ultimate cause which is itself causeless.

The original Shri Shankara is best known for his work, "The Crest Jewel of Discrimination" (Vivekachudamani), that forms the basis of the non-dual advaita philosophy. Here the nature of discrimination is described as the ability to see beyond the consensus view that we have of ourselves and the world, to the ultimate reality. He quotes the simile from the Upanishads of the piece of rope that is mistaken for a snake: with the light of reason its true nature is seen, and all fear goes. This mistaken view relates to the way we see ourselves as being separate individuals and hence separate 'doers' of our actions and the larger external world as being separate and external from ourselves instead of being experienced as a single unity.

There are two stages in the discriminatory process. The first involves separating what is 'Self' from what is 'not Self'. In other words, separating what is transitory from what is eternal. We give up our identity with all that belongs to the line of time and identify with the still, unchanging centre of our Being which is beyond sensations, perceptions and thought processes.

This is a necessary first stage. Otherwise our identity just remains at the level of the drama on the line of passing time, and all that that entails.

The second stage of Viveka, or discrimination, involves realising that the Self is not just the still unchanging centre of our being but is manifesting as everything we perceive. Even all the changing aspects of the drama of life, creation, maintenance and destruction, birth and death, illness and health, the saint and the sinner alike, all are aspects of the One. Or, as Rumi put it:

> "The whole sum of pictured forms is a mere reflection in the water of the river:
> When you rub your eye, you will perceive that all of them are really He."

In Buddhism we find the same concept expressed by the word, 'prajna' or 'discriminative wisdom', often symbolised by the sword held by the deity, Manjusri. Here also there is no concept of adding anything new but simply the use of the discriminative reason to cut away ignorance, false modes of perception and identity until, like the analogy of the snake and the rope, we perceive reality as it is and always has been.

In the world's non-dual traditions emphasis is put on the fact that non-duality is not a state that the universe is evolving towards but is a situation that already exists. Non-duality is a state which exists 'now' so that whatever comes before us is 'it'. The sharp sword of discriminative wisdom is needed to cut away the discursive mind that continually takes us away from this present moment awareness and deprives us of our innate ability to see the world as it already is.

So how does the concept of 'Viveka' have a practical effect on our actions in our daily lives?

With the realisation that we are all just aspects of the One Self, our actions are naturally modified in accordance with this realisation so that, rather than being artificially curbed from below, we start to reflect the One Universal Nature from above. We witness the One Universal Nature manifesting in our thoughts, words and deeds.

Quotations:

> *"The rise of the Viveka is only possible through discoursing with a Realised Man or discoursing with those who are wiser than you. Discoursing and trying to get at the Truth about things will bring Viveka."*
>
> *The Shankaracharya*

"A firm conviction of the mind to the effect that Brahman is real and the universe is unreal, is designated as the discrimination (Viveka) between the Real and the unreal.

To remove his bondage the wise man should discriminate between the Self and the non-Self. By that alone he comes to know his own Self as Existence-Knowledge-Bliss Absolute, and becomes happy.

He indeed is free who discriminates between all sense-objects and the indwelling, unattached and inactive Self, as one separates a stalk of grass from its enveloping sheath, and merging everything in It remains in a state of identity with That." *Shankara*

"An eye that can penetrate the cause is needed to extirpate these veils from root and bottom, so that it may behold the Causer in the world of non-spatiality and regard exertion and earnings and shops as mere nonsense. Everything good or evil comes from the Causer: causes and means, O father, are naught but a phantom that has materialised on the King's highway in order that the reign of ignorance may endure for some little time."[3] *Rumi*

"The perception of a phenomenon is the perception of the Universal Nature, since phenomena and Mind are one and the same. It is only because you cling to outward forms that you come to 'see', 'hear', 'feel' and 'know' things as individual entities. True perception is beyond your powers so long as you indulge in these."[20] *Huang Po*

"Our original Buddha-Nature is, in highest truth, devoid of any atom of objectivity. It is void, omnipresent, silent, pure; it is glorious and mysterious peaceful joy - and that is all. Enter deeply into it by awaking to it yourself. That which is before you is it, in all its fullness, utterly complete. There is naught beside. Even if you go through all the stages of a Bodhisattva's progress towards Buddhahood, one by one; when at last, in a single flash, you attain to full realization, you will only be realizing the Buddha-Nature which has been with you all the time; and by all the foregoing stages

you will have added to it nothing at all. You will come to look upon those aeons of work and achievement as no better than unreal actions performed in a dream."[20]

Huang Po

"As a thing is viewed, so it appears. To see things as a multiplicity, and so to cleave unto separateness, is to err."

Padmasambhava

"Away with your dualism, your likes and dislikes. Every single thing is just the One Mind. When you have perceived this, you will have mounted the Chariot of the Buddhas."[20]

Huang Po

"There is no reaching the Self. If Self were to be reached, it would mean that the Self is not here and now and that it is yet to be obtained. What is got afresh will also be lost. So it will be impermanent. What is not permanent is not worth striving for. So I say the Self is not reached. You are the Self, you are already that.

The fact is, you are ignorant of your blissful state. Ignorance supervenes and draws a veil over the pure Self which is bliss. Attempts are directed only to remove this veil of ignorance which is merely wrong knowledge. The wrong knowledge is the false identification of the Self with the body and the mind. This false identification must go, and then the Self alone remains.

Therefore realisation is for everyone; realisation makes no difference between the aspirants. This very doubt, whether you can realise, and the notion 'I-have-not-realised' are themselves the obstacles. Be free from these obstacles also."[21]

Ramana Maharshi

"His disciples said to Him, 'When will the repose of the dead come about and when will the new world come?'
He said to them, 'What you look forward to has already come, but you do not recognise it'"[22]

The Gospel of Thomas

"The Realisation of the Non dual traditions is uncompromising: there is only Spirit, there is only God, there is only Emptiness in all its radiant wonder. All the good and all the evil, the very best and the very worst, the upright and the degenerate - each and all are radically perfect manifestations of spirit precisely as they are. There is nothing but God, nothing but the Goddess, nothing but spirit in all directions, and not a grain of sand, nor a speck of dust, is more or less spirit than any other."[5] *Ken Wilber*

"We want to think about Param-Atman. As it is the source of all greatness, its own greatness must be infinite. As it is the source of all happiness, its own happiness must be boundless. As it is the source of all beauty, its own beauty must be - we do not know ....But how could we ever think about such a Param Atman whose qualities and nature are thus beyond the utmost stretch of human imagination?

This was the question which was naturally put by Arjuna to the Lord Krishna, and the answer is contained in the Bhagavad Gita, chapter 10, verses 20 to 42.

Here is a translation of a few of those verses:

> *"O Arjuna! I am the Self, seated in the hearts of all beings; I am the beginning, and the life and I am the end of them all.*
>
> *Of the scriptures I am the hymns; I am the electric force in the powers of nature; of the senses, I am the registering mind; and I am the intelligence in all that lives.*
>
> *Among the vital forces I am life itself; I am Mammon to the heathen and godless; I am energy in fire, earth, wind, heaven, sun, moon and planets ...*
>
> *I am all-devouring Death; I am the origin of all that may happen; I am fame, fortune, speech, memory, intellect, constancy and forgiveness.*

I am the gambling of the cheat, and the splendour of the splendid; I am victory; I am effort; I am the purity of the pure ....

Whatever is glorious, excellent, beautiful or mighty, be assured that it comes from only a part of My splendour.

But what is the use of all these details to you? O Arjuna! I sustain all this world with only a fragment of Myself."

All this implies that by thinking of the most powerful manifest thing as only a tiny particle of Param-Atman's power; by thinking of the most beautiful object we can, and then treating it as a mere atom of the Param-Atman's beauty, and so on, we can gradually find our way to the Param-Atman. Thus, starting from sensory objects and rising higher and higher, we reach a state where all difference between sensory and ultrasensory, between definable and indefinable has faded away from us.

Then, what to ordinary people are different forms and shapes, are to a Fully-Realised person all manifestations of one and the same Param-Atman. What he sees then, around himself and within himself, is Param-Atman, and not the mirage which we call "the world". Such a man would welcome heat and cold, pleasure and pain, fortune and misfortune - all alike, because all are manifestations of Param-Atman."

The Shankaracharya

Part Twenty Two

LIFE AS A JOURNEY

One of the main metaphors used in this framework is Rumi's story of the man from Baghdad who dreamt of a great treasure in a particular house in Cairo. After a long journey he arrived in Cairo and found the house. There he met a man who had dreamt about a great treasure in a house in Baghdad. The first man recognised the house in Baghdad as his own and on returning there found that the treasure was hidden there all the time.

This is similar to the parable of the Prodigal Son in the Gospels. This story tells how a man left his father's house and went out into the world with his inheritance. Eventually, having spent all his money and in a state of destitution he 'comes to himself' and remembers the existence of his father's house and begins the return journey. His father sees him from afar and runs out to meet him.

Both of these stories suggest that we are already in possession of a great treasure but in order to become aware of its existence it is necessary to set out on the journey of life and to say 'yes' to its experiences. It can seem paradoxical that we are already the One Consciousness and yet we set out on the journey of life to rediscover this principle in a much fuller way. So what exactly is the nature of this treasure? How do we forget it? And how do we rediscover it?

The treasure is surely our own true Self, our own basic sense of 'I Am' that is always present as the ground of our awareness. We forget the existence of this treasure because, for the purposes and manifestation of the drama of life, Consciousness identifies with form. Rather than identify with the pure 'I Am' we identify our sense of 'amness' with the vehicle of consciousness and its life story. For example we may say "I am rich" or "I am poor" or "I am successful" or "I am unsuccessful" or anything else that defines our identity at the level of the drama of life. In this way, as we build up our lives in the world, we define our identity by what we are and what we do, by our sex, our race, our position in society, our job title and so on.

As we pass through life many of these identities fall away, often as a result of events we may regard as tragedies, such as illness, redundancy or bereavement. As these lesser levels of identity fall away we can start to become aware of our true identity, the 'I Am' that has always been present but which is beyond categorisation or definition. It is the very thing we have always wanted and sought after all our lives, often without realising it.

As our awareness of this true identify arises we may find ourselves with what Ken Wilber refers to as "a new duty in Consciousness", a role in the drama that is not based on any sense of individual doership, identity or position in life but is the outflowing of this true Self as it manifests from moment to moment.

It is often reported that when people set out on a spiritual path there can be some quite intense experiences which act as a sort of 'incentive bonus'. As one progresses these can become less so that the aspirant is forced to trust and depend on his or her own inner reserves. This can cause some people to move from path to path just to have this honeymoon period again and again. But if we persist and the journey nears its end, we see that we have never ever been separate from this great treasure that is our own true Self.

Quotations:

"It doesn't matter how lonely you are: it doesn't matter how bad the situation is, or how hopeless the outlook; it's just that lesser values have to be broken down until one finds this thing in all our hearts which is God and Love and Truth and one's Self all at the same time." *Dr Roles*

"Let peace and satisfaction be with you. My blessings are with you. You are not alone, for the bond between the disciple and the teacher is eternal. If you prefer to call this suffering, we are all in it. All lives are governed by laws. The body is just a manifestation of our essence. With the first breath of life, we inherit a complete pattern of the physical body. Practically everything is destined for it. Those who walk into a School and undergo discipline have the good fortune of improving upon the subtle body which establish-

es the pattern for the next life. The physical body must fulfil whatever has been destined for it. Common men or women rejoice in pleasure and cry in pain. Initiates know that they are not the body, so whatever happens to the body is just allowed to happen without pleasure or pain. The Atman, and even the subtle body, is not subject to the sufferings of the physical body. This understanding gives them a different attitude which nullifies the pain of the suffering. The suffering is part of the plan. When the subtle body is getting purer, the impurities reflect as suffering on the physical body. This is in fact a testing time as well as paying off time. Make sure the pain doesn't seem to affect the real Being. Miracles are possible, but a miracle only postpones the situation, or makes someone else pay for the other, thus miracles are very undesirable things. The greatest miracle of all is the true understanding of the situation. You are not in pain because you are not the body. Live happily and live in the present. The past is dead and the future is full of mercy of the Lord." *The Shankaracharya*

"The first decade is spent mostly learning to live in the world with grown-ups. The second decade is spent making discoveries for oneself and about oneself. The next decades, the third, fourth and fifth are mostly spent on just keeping going - working, a career, bringing up a family, fulfilling all the various obligations of life. It is often hard to find energy for anything else. In the sixth and seventh decades we ease up a little. The opportunities are there. This is when one sees that everything has been provided by Param-Atman. So in the last decade, we prepare for the next stage of the journey, thanking Param-Atman for the gift of life."
Dr Roles

"The teachings tell us what it is we need to realise, but we also have to go on our own journey, in order to come to a personal realisation. That journey may take us through suffering, difficulties, and doubts of all kinds, but they will become our greatest teachers. Through them we will learn the humility to recognise our limitations, and through them

we will discover the inner strength and fearlessness we need to emerge from our old habits and set patterns, and surrender into the vaster vision of real freedom offered by the spiritual teachings."[23] *Sogyol Rimpoche*

"Unless something breaks down your normal conventional world, you can't get beyond, and that's why sickness, pain, loss, all these things are positive values, if you learn to accept them, and I'm told that when people are dying they resent it at first very much and fight against it and get so angry, but the moment they learn to accept it, to see it's the will of God, it's the way things are, they can be totally transformed. You let yourself go then something deeper takes over and transforms you .... and often the most painful loss of a wife or a child, or an accident, or whatever, is the way in which you open yourself to the divine.

Bede Griffiths, Colet House 9.4.92

"When the Great Search is undone, and the separate self sense has been crucified; when the continuity of witnessing has stabilised in our own case; when ever-present awareness is your constant ground - then your entire bodymind will regenerate, resurrect, and reorganise itself around intrinsic Spirit, and you will arise, as from the dead, to a new destiny and a new duty in consciousness.

And whatever the form of your own resurrection, you will arise, driven not by the Great Search, but by your own Great Duty, your limitless Dharma, the manifestation of your own highest potentials, and the world will begin to change, because of you. And you will never flinch, and you will never fail in that great Duty, and you will never turn away, because simple, ever-present awareness will be with you now and forever, even unto the ends of the worlds, because now and forever and endlessly forever, there is only Spirit, only intrinsic awareness, only the simple awareness of just this and nothing more."[5] *Ken Wilber*

".....If the person insists on a certain program, and doesn't listen to the demands of his own heart, he's going to risk a

schizophrenic crack up. Such a person has put himself off centre. He has aligned himself with a program for life, and it's not the one the body's interested in at all. The world is full of people who have stopped listening to themselves, or have listened only to their neighbours to learn what they ought to do, how they out to behave, and what the values are that they should be living for."[1] *Joseph Campbell*

"Rise up and awake out of sleep, and hearken unto the words of the letter.
and remember that thou art a son of kings:
lo, thou hast come under the yoke of bondage.
Remember the pearl for which thou wast sent
into Egypt.
Remember thy garment spangled with gold,
and the glorious mantle which thou shouldest
wear and wherewith thou shouldest deck thyself.
Thy name is named in the book of life."[24]

Acts of Thomas

"To me, nurturing the soul is a simple matter of honouring my process, of trusting in and turning my life over to what the Higher Power has in mind for me. Whenever I fight my process, I'm miserable. Instead of struggling, I need to ask every day, "what do You have in mind for me today?" Then I accept the answer trusting it, rather than fighting to control my life."[25] *Anne Wilson Schaef*

"I think each one must follow his own light, whether you are a Hindu or a Buddhist or an atheist. An atheist has his own understanding of truth and justice. You must follow the light and keep open to wherever the light leads you. The one demand on all of us is to be true to the inner Self, the inner light within, and that will lead you to your goal, whatever it may be." *Bede Griffiths*

Part Twenty Three

GAPS

In the study of Purusha and Prakriti or "Stillness and Manifestation" we saw that there are two aspects of creation: the still, unmanifest consciousness and the manifest universe which is the expression of that Consciousness. We saw, too, how there are times when the curtain parts and we become aware of this underlying stillness.

In this paper we will look closer at these moments of stillness and how we can become more aware of them. The writer Eckhart Tolle uses the phrase "portals into the unmanifest" to describe these moments of opportunity.

In the Advaita tradition there is the concept of 'gaps between desires', moments between one set of motivations and another, between one set of actions and another that are provided by nature when we can naturally rest in this silent awareness. It is not a question of doing anything at these times but simply becoming aware of 'not doing' and an awareness of 'Being'. In our normal waking state of physical and mental activity we tend to pass these moments by but once we do start to notice them they become more frequent.

There are a number of other portals or gaps naturally provided in life. One is the deep sleep state. As we go to sleep at night, after the cessation of physical activity, we pass through a subtle world of mental activity in the form of dreams and come to rest in the causal world of deep and dreamless sleep. It is a realm of no experience, no sense of separation and no sense of time. In the morning the process is reversed and we awake with renewed energy to embark on our day's activities.

Another portal is provided in deep meditation. Unlike deep sleep, which is entered into unconsciously, this state is entered into consciously as thought processes are transcended. In order for this to happen during a period of meditation it is necessary not just to become caught up with the technique itself but to pass beyond to the great stillness to which it points. As with deep sleep there is no experience at this level. You only know about it afterwards as your being is suffused with a great sense of deep peace and a quiet inner happiness.

Another portal which can open up in our lives results from the experience of awe and wonder. This can happen when we are confronted with intense beauty whether it is in the natural world or as a result of art or music. This portal can also open up at times of great emergency or intense grief. In both cases the only response can be for the moving mind to fall silent as we momentarily step behind the curtain of the phenomenal display of life into an awareness of the unmanifest reality that underpins it.

There is a further portal that awaits us and that is the moment of death of the physical body.

In some traditions the process of birth and death is said to be the same process as falling asleep at night and waking in the morning. At birth we pass from the undifferentiated unity of the Divine and Causal level through the subtle to a manifest physical body. At death the process is reversed as we let go of lesser levels of identity and return back to the great unmanifest.

The importance of having an awareness of these gaps or portals in our lives is that it prepares us for this ultimate moment of letting go. There is a Sufi saying that suggests that if we die before we die we will not taste death.

Every time we become aware of a gap we are dying to lesser levels of identity and acknowledging our true "I AM" that is always present and exists prior to birth and after death. As we persist it is no longer a question of isolated gaps, for this state of "Amness" or presence starts to become our background state of awareness. No matter what is happening in our lives, whether we are active or at rest, thinking or still, it is always there in the background silently watching.

Quotations:

> *"Every individual has desires, and we are plagued with these desires, but there is some time between each of them. Most of the time we do not allow this interval to stretch at all; no sooner is one desire fulfilled than we let another*

desire spring up. If people understood this and allowed themselves the luxury of a little interval, however short it might be, they would find that they would re-charge themselves without doing anything but just being quiet for a moment or two. If people could practise this and enlarge this interval - say up to five minutes at one stretch - they would find that they had great power within, and the potentiality of realising themselves would not be far off if they could do this, giving themselves the luxury of two minutes of interval between one desire and the rising of the next."

The Shankaracharya

"When your consciousness is directed outward, mind and world arise. When it is directed inward, it realizes its own Source and returns home into the Unmanifested."[26]

Eckhart Tolle

"Fix your heart on stillness. We achieve stillness on the physical level in sleep at night; stillness on the subtle level (our psychology) is to prolong the time between desires - between the fulfillment of one desire and the start of the next; fulfillment and stillness on the causal level is something to which the meditation should be taking us for one or two moments each half hour; and two moments of stillness on the causal level would supply us with energy for twenty-four hours after. We must not expect more than a moment or two. The whole half hour is to try to get those two moments of complete stillness." *Dr Roles*

"The refusal to let go of our projects at times and of our projections feeds our temptations to climb, for climbing has a projected goal known as "the top of the ladder". The Via Negativa teaches us that sinking is more holy than climbing. Depth is more godlike than height. The Creator God, a great underground river, awaits our sinking more than our climbing. The reason we can trust the sinking so deeply is that, at the bottom, "my ground and God's are the same." (Eckhart) God is already at home in a deep, deep way. But we need to return home to make contact with that depth. As

Eckhart puts it, "God is at home; it is we who have gone out for a walk." The Via Negativa is about returning home. Sin is about our missing the mark, wandering about in superficial or "outer" fashion of living".[27] *Matthew Fox*

"During the night after a serious operation I was aware of being above myself looking down at my body lying on the bed, nurses and doctors leaning over, checking blood pressure and blood transfusion. My 'mind' seemed then to be travelling down a long corridor at the very end of which a brilliant yellow light shone. I was filled with elation and pure joy. The nearest description of the feeling was what I felt as a child on the last day of the summer term, knowing that six weeks' holiday loomed ahead full of freedom and sunshine. I felt absolutely no fear at all, just utter pleasure, as if I was off somewhere wonderful. It was therefore with some astonishment that I awoke to find myself still in a hospital bed and very much earthbound. I cannot tell you how long I was in my state of bliss and I have never experienced anything like it since."[28] *Near Death Experience*

"The pain was replaced by this wonderful feeling, such a contrast to the pain and suffering; I was convinced no living person could experience such joy. The only way I can explain it is think of the happiest moment of your life, and when you do, that happiest moment is awful pain compared to what you feel, and I will swear to that. You really want to stay where you are, even though you are aware something has changed or is changing. I'm convinced it was only my family that really brought me back. If I live for a thousand years I will remember it. Religion, no matter what denomination, plays no part in it whatsoever. I would like to encourage people to be unafraid of death. I have a completely different attitude to life after death after my experience."[28] *Near Death Experience*

"I wasn't sure when the light in the room began to change; suddenly I was aware that it was brighter, a lot brighter, than it had been. I whirled to look at the night-light on the

bedside table. Surely a single 15-watt bulb couldn't turn out that much light!

I stared in astonishment as the brightness increased, coming from nowhere, seeming to shine everywhere at once ..... Far more even than power, what emanated from this presence was unconditioned love. An astonishing love. A love beyond my wildest imagining. This love knew every unlovable thing about me - the quarrels with my step-mother, my explosive temper, the sex thoughts I could never control, every mean, selfish thought and action since the day I was born - and accepted and loved me just the same."[29]

George Ritchie

"To work with changes now, in life: That is the real way to prepare for death. Life may be full of pain, suffering and difficulty, but all of these are opportunities handed to us to help us move toward an emotional acceptance of death. It is only when we believe things to be permanent that we shut off the possibility of learning from change."[23]

Sogyol Rimpoche

"If, at the moment of death, you can unite your mind confidently with the wisdom mind of the master and die in that peace, then all, I promise and assure you, will be well.

Our task in life is to practice this merging with the wisdom mind of the master again and again, so that it becomes so natural that every activity - sitting, walking, eating, drinking, sleeping, dreaming and waking - starts to be increasingly permeated by the master's living presence. Slowly, over years of focused devotion, you begin to know and realise, all appearances to be the display of the wisdom of the master. All the situations of life, even those that once seemed tragic, meaningless, or terrifying, reveal themselves more and more transparently to be the direct teaching and blessing of the master, and the inner teacher."[23]

Sogyol Rinpoche

"Pat had a second stroke a year later ... it seemed that,

according to the doctors, he had actually died during this attack for a time, but had managed to pull himself back into life because he felt he had one more message to deliver. Death, he told us, was nothing to fear. It was a natural culmination to life as we know it and was an experience of indescribable happiness. The release from the bondage of life - even from the bondage of love - brought with it an ecstasy and an understanding beyond anything known to living man." *"Life of Sir Patrick Hastings"*

Part Twenty Four

PARADOX

There are several aspects of the non-dual teaching that can appear contradictory and paradoxical. In this chapter we shall look at some of the probable reasons why the teaching can appear like this at times.

We have already seen how it is impossible to understand non-dualism with just the rational mind and thus it can appear paradoxical not because it is so but because this is how reality can appear when viewed from a limited perspective. In order to come close to the non-dual perspective it is necessary to suspend the ordinary analytical mind with its judgements of like or dislike, good or bad etc. and view phenomena from a point of stillness without the judgements that normally colour our perception and which spring from a separate sense of self.

Another aspect of the teaching that can give rise to paradox is when an artificial duality is created "for the purposes of training". An example of this is the concept of Atman and Paramatman, used to signify an apparent difference between the individual and the Universal Divine Self when in reality there is only one Divine Self which includes everything. As we saw in the chapter on 'Viveka' it is first necessary to go inwards in stillness to find our own inner reality before we discover that this is not just our own inner reality but is manifesting as everything we perceive. In this way many of the concepts in Advaita are seen to be metaphors intended to point the way but which can be discarded when reality is perceived at first hand.

There is yet another concept in Advaita that can lead to paradox and that is the teaching on the four levels. It possible to view phenomena and events from the perspective of each level. For example, from the point of view of the physical and subtle levels we appear to be separate entities acting on an external world and reacting with other separate entities. From the point of view of our daily lives it is necessary to act 'as if' this is so and to try to play our parts as best we can. When these same events are viewed from the perspective of the Divine level all separation vanishes and instead of separate entities the perception is of One Universal Self playing all the varied roles in the drama. In this way the concept of the four levels is seen to be just another metaphor. In reality all that exists is the Divine level. We only perceive separate levels when we identify our sense of self with less than who we really are. When we identify with our true "I AM" the world of multiplicity vanishes and all is experienced as Divine.

So it is necessary to act and live 'as if' it is a world of multiplicity and 'as if' one is a separate doer but at the back of one's mind is the realisation that it is all a great show staged by and acted by the Universal.

When we talk about the world or ourselves it is necessary to be clear about the level we are talking from. We also need to remember that the Divine level perspective is the fullest reality. Confusion can arise when we use the cognition of one level to understand a different level, a phenomenon that Ken Wilber refers to as "category error". For example, when dealing with cases of bereavement or illness, sympathy, understanding and practical help is usually more appropriate than talk about the perfect world or the non-dual reality.

There is a further concept that gives rise to paradox in the non-dual model. We have seen how creation is the manifest unfolding of the Universal Consciousness and is complete at every moment and yet, in some traditions, the life of humanity is described as being subject to a series of developmental stages as if the spectrum of four levels is laid out horizontally along the line of time with humanity gradually progressing through these different stages as Consciousness seeks to know itself through its own Creation. Or, as Rumi puts it:

> "Humankind is being led along an evolving course,
> through this migration of intelligences
> and though we seem to be sleeping
> there is an inner wakefulness
> that directs the dream
> and that will eventually startle us back
> to the truth of who we are."

Within the non-dual traditions part of the teaching deals with the inner aspect of awakening from the dream of separation and liberation from the cycle of birth and death. However, there is often another part that deals with the general evolution of consciousness on the larger scale of humanity and the establishment of justice and equity in the world. Realised men and associated organisations often have a role to play within this aspect of the drama.

In coming to understand non-duality more fully it is necessary to allow these different aspects of the teaching to sit side by side without feeling any sense of conflict or contradiction. It is also necessary to be aware that ultimately the whole drama of creation and all the different aspects of life we encounter and our different reactions are all just the unfolding of the 'One Mind' in whom we "live, move and have our Being".

Quotations:

> *"Here is a story about that from the Shankaracharya, our Meditation guide, who always takes a very optimistic view of things when seen on a larger scale.*
>
> > *In that famous Indian epic, the Ramayana, written by a contemporary of our Shakespeare, is described a King of the Dynasty of the Sun who had two boys Rama and Lakshman. Rama grew up to be the perfect man (all that a man could be) and his younger brother Lakshman was also perfect but lived in comparative ignorance. When he was a little boy, living in the palace, the Lord Chamberlain came to the King one day and said, "Your little son Lakshman is in a frightful mood today! He is in a very bad temper and has just broken all the glass chandeliers in the palace." The King said, "I think that's rather fun, let's have a feast." Much upset, the Lord Chamberlain said, "What do you mean? Do you really appreciate what that bad boy has been doing?" The King answered, "But don't you think it's fine that he's got that strong; he couldn't have done all that a year or two ago." So he celebrated the event with a feast!*

And in fact, mankind is reckoned to have only lived quite a short part of his life - just a few million years out of the three thousand million years that life has existed on the earth - and he can be considered as being like the inky schoolboy right now, who is rather a danger to himself, may blow himself up now and then, but who'll get older and grow out of it! We don't believe that this is the end of civilisation, the end of humanity, or anything grand like that; one civilisation may be giving place to another but it won't affect the earth or the solar system. Is that all right by you?

Dr Roles

Part Twenty Five

"NOT TWO"

The word "Advaita" or "Non-Duality" literally means 'not two'. It implies that everything is an aspect of One Universal Consciousness or undivided whole.

Whilst it is a profoundly simple concept, so simple in fact that we tend to miss its significance, it is also a concept that is impossible to understand using the rational intellect alone. It is more a question of direct experience.

As we saw in the chapter on Viveka part of the difficulty in understanding non-duality is that in our thinking we tend not to go far enough back in the chain of causality. As a result we are left with a model of reality that is still dualistic. This is due, in part, to our deeply ingrained dualistic ways of viewing the world and phenomena. It is very easy to be like the ants who lived on the salt mountain who, when they were led to the sugar mountain, were unable to taste the sweet sugar because they had kept a little salt in their mouths.

It is often difficult, for example, to go beyond the duality of "God and man" or "the Creator and his Creation". Due to habitual thought patterns we often see these as separate entities with a multitude of separate wills interacting with each other rather than seeing them as variable aspects of one Whole with just one Will.

It is understandable that we sometimes find this a difficult concept to accept for when we look around us events in the world appear to unfold in a way which is very different to our own ideas of justice. We are then rather like Job in the Bible who berates God for all the injustices he sees happening to him. God answers Job by asking him where he was when He created the world. He then gives a lengthy discourse on Job's inability to understand the plan of creation from his limited ego perspective.

This is similar to the view expressed by the Oxford theologian, Keith Ward, during a talk given at Colet House when he emphasised our inability to understand the will and purpose of the

Creator from a limited personal perspective. Yet we often presume to know how God should act, "teaching the Creator his business" as Dr Roles once called it.

We are, however, as aspects of the unfolding of the One Consciousness, able to respond appropriately to what is before us at any moment according to our role in the drama. This may include taking action to fight injustice wherever we see it and being magnanimous and compassionate in all our dealings with our fellow men and our environment.

So it is necessary to back up our understanding to the non-dual perspective of a Unity that contains no opposites and then view the world, ourselves and all phenomena from this viewpoint. Sometimes we may find this easy but at other times, perhaps when we are having a difficult time in our lives or an event happens in the world that we cannot understand, it is not so easy.

The main purpose of "satsang", or meeting together, is to inspire each other and remind each other of the all-pervasiveness of the Self. This is especially necessary at times when we may have forgotten and become immersed in life's drama so that our thinking has become fragmented. Through this process our ingrained tendencies of dualistic reasoning are gradually chipped away, bit by bit. It is then rather like the way in which the sun tries to break through on a misty morning: it makes several attempts but the mist reasserts itself until finally, as if 'the penny has dropped', the sun breaks through and all the mist dissolves never to return.

Quotations:

> *"If God did not answer his unanswerable human question about suffering and grief it was at least a rather special sort of 'no' answer, more like a silent certainly not uncompassionate gaze. As though he shook his head not in refusal but waiving the question: like "Peace child you don't understand".*[30] *Brian Sibley*

> *"The Being of God remains beyond all perceptions. Now what's the importance of that? It is to say that you never grasp what the Divine Mind really is. You are confined to a world of pictures constructed from your personality, your*

imagination interacting with that truly unknowable Reality which is God but which is the Reality underlying all the things of space and time, always present. I think that resolves some of the all too superficial questions that people raise about God like, "How can God allow terrible evils in the world?" That's because they've got an idea of what God is and then they look at the evils in the world and say, "Oh my idea doesn't fit that and therefore there's no God" whereas what they should say is, "My idea is wrong". If what I'm trying to find out is the nature of the Mind underlying the universe, the Reality underlying appearances, I've got to take appearances at full face, the way they are. They are terrifying, they are dangerous, they are beautiful, they are marvellous, they are both. So the Mind underlying the universe must be both.

This is much more straightforward in the Indian tradition actually where, of course, the Mind of the universe is terrifying and terrible. The vision of Krishna which occurs in the Bhagavad Gita is a terrible horrifying vision of a Being who devours millions of human beings with their mangled bodies entangled in its teeth, not a loving, heavenly father. It is in fact time which brings decay and death and destruction to all things. Then, of course, Arjuna says, "Oh stop that vision. I don't like that. Let's go back to just seeing nice Krishna standing in the chariot."

These are both images of the Divine Mind and we would be wrong to reject either so I think there is a sense in which you could say, "God is love" but it's a very careful sense, and its not the way that the Mind of the Universe actually appears. I think the way it actually appears is a way I would describe as one of beautiful terror. And that's the way the universe appears to most of us. But remember that the way it appears to us is the way it is because of what we are. And there may be a state to which we attain, in which the Reality behind that Universe, the Mind of the Cosmos itself, is something beyond beauty and terror, something we can only dimly envisage, something we are working towards."

Keith Ward talk at Colet House 2005

"Think of the most beautiful person you have ever seen. Think of the exact moment you looked into his or her eyes, and for a fleeting second you were paralysed: you couldn't take you eyes off that vision. You stared, frozen in time, caught in that beauty. Now imagine that identical beauty radiating from every single thing in the entire universe: every rock, every plant, every animal, every cloud, every person, every object, every mountain, every stream - even the garbage dumps and broken dreams - every single one of them, radiating that beauty. You are quietly frozen by the gentle beauty of everything that arises around you. You are released from grasping, released from time, released from avoidance, released altogether into the eye of Spirit where you contemplate the unending beauty of the Art that is the entire world."[5] *Ken Wilber*

"The manifested and phenomenal world is primarily based on Chit, which is Consciousness. This Consciousness is also known at Atman ..The phenomenal world, or the world of name and form, is practically reduced to the five elements, or one can say that these five elements are manipulated in such a way that they give rise to these multifarious forms and multiple names. One may ask where these elements come from? They have their origin in Prakriti, Nature, the base of which is Atman, for it is the nature of the Atman which is taking different forms. Atman is the cause of everything and itself ... If one goes on seeking the chain of cause and effect, one finds Atman as the ultimate cause, which is itself causeless. Thus the basis of all the names and forms is the consciousness of Atman."

The Shankaracharya

Part Twenty Six

A COMPLETE CHANGE OF VIEW

The implications of the non-dual model are very far reaching in their effect on the way we view ourselves, our lives and the world.

From the point of view of this model we are all parts of the manifestation of One Being where everything is in exactly the right place and in the only place possible at each moment. It is much like a vast multi-dimensional jigsaw where all the different aspects of creation, including those things that appear on the surface as opposites, dovetail together to form one unified whole.

Think about that for a while and all that it entails. It includes the clouds and the birds in the sky, the fish in the sea, all the waving stems of grass in the wind, the billions of people of all nations, the insects and atoms, all the stars in our Milky Way, the two hundred billion galaxies in the Universe, all inseparable aspects of One Being. There is not an atom out of place, it is all the manifestation of Spirit down to the smallest detail. Yet we tend to perceive ourselves as separate entities, each with a separate will acting on a separate world trying to manipulate it to go our way. From this viewpoint we are like a speck in a vast mechanical universe. This view of the world and of ourselves is as upside-down and back-to-front as it is possible to be.

The work of Self Realisation involves turning around these mistaken concepts. This is not always easy since we have become identified with the vehicle of Consciousness, the mind-body mechanism, rather than with Consciousness itself.

This mistaken identity is sometimes referred to as "false I" or "false ego". The "true I" or ego is our identity with the Universal, our basic sense of "I AM" that is always available in the Now.

The importance of acknowledging the all pervasiveness of the One Consciousness is that it dissolves this false identity at its source. Our identity at this level is often defined by the events that have happened to us in life and our life story, and it is partly kept in place by our identification with suffering. For example, it is easy to recognise the victim mentality in others and even oneself at times! There may be times when we feel we have been wronged or betrayed. It is often these hurts and the feeling of being the one in the right that reinforces this sense of being a separate ego rather than an inseparable aspect of one whole.

One way to let go of this false identity is the realisation that other people are also the manifestation of Consciousness. Then automatically forgiveness starts to arise. For how is it possible to blame Consciousness? Was not that other person also playing their role in the drama?

With this realisation the events in life begin to become less important than our reaction to them. Life takes on the quality of being a process of transformation. We begin to become aware of our identity as the witness of the drama rather than as a participator.

Life, by its very nature, will present us with an ever-changing cycle of events which, as well as happiness, will inevitably include pain and loss. By changing our view right around to one of accepting the all pervasiveness of the Universal Consciousness, the transformation of our attitudes takes place from above by the simple process of acknowledging the ultimate Source. Because this means turning around some very deep seated attitudes, it is not usually an immediate process. For a while we may swing back and forth between these two views: seeing the world and everything in it as separate and random, and seeing everything as an aspect of one whole.

From this latter viewpoint events that we had previously perceived as difficult or negative start to change their nature. They are now seen as stepping stones or reminders that take us back into the acknowledgement of our true and ever-present identity.

Quotations

"At one time there was a demon known as Rakshu who was fighting with Indra. At one stage of the fight, when he was distracted, Indra's sword slipped out of his hand. Being disarmed, he was afraid that Rakshu would kill him. At this point Rakshu said "Don't worry! It is all a theatrical affair that we are fighting and you have been given this job to fight me, so pick up your own sword again and then we will go on

fighting, you needn't be afraid." *The Shankaracharya*

"That's right. Schopenhauer, in his splendid essay called, "On an Apparent Intention in the Fate of the Individual," points out that when you reach an advanced age and look back over your lifetime, it can seem to have had a consistent order and plan, as though composed by some novelist. Events that when they occurred had seemed accidental and of little moment turn out to have been indispensable factors in the composition of a consistent plot. So who composed that plot? Schopenhauer suggests that just as your dreams are composed by an aspect of yourself of which your consciousness is unaware, so, too, your whole life is composed by the will within you. And just as people whom you will have met apparently by mere chance became leading agents in the structuring of your life, so, too, will you have served unknowingly as an agent, giving meaning to the lives of others. The whole thing gears together like one big symphony, with everything unconsciously structuring everything else. And Schopenhauer concludes that it is as though our lives were the features of the one great dream of a single dreamer in which all the dream characters dream, too; so that everything links to everything else, moved by the one will to life which is the universal will in nature.

It's a magnificent idea - an idea that appears in India in the mythic image of the Net of Indra, which is a net of gems, where at every crossing of one thread over another there is a gem reflecting all the other reflective gems. Everything arises in mutual relation to everything else, so you can't blame anybody for anything. It is even as though there were a single intention behind it all, which always makes some kind of sense, though none of us knows what the sense might be, or has lived the life that he quite intended."[1]

Joseph Campbell

"What is it then to be stable? It seems to me that it may be described in the following terms: you will find stability at the moment when you discover that God is everywhere, that you do not need to seek Him elsewhere, that He is here, and if you do not find Him here it is useless to go and search for

Him elsewhere because it is not Him that is absent from us, it is we who are absent from Him ... it is important to recognise that it is useless to seek God somewhere else. If you cannot find Him here you will not find Him anywhere else. This is important because it is only at the moment that you recognise this that you can truly find the fullness of the Kingdom of God in all its richness within you; that God is present in every situation and every place, that you will be able to say; 'so then I shall stay where I am'."

Metropolitan Anthony Bloom

"So you are not in here, on this side of a transparent window, looking at the Kosmos out there. The transparent window has shattered, your bodymind drops, you are free of that confinement forever, you are no longer "behind your face" looking at the Kosmos - you simply are the Kosmos. You are all that. Which is precisely why you can swallow the Kosmos and span the centuries, and nothing moves at all. The sound of this one hand clapping is the sound the Big Bang made. It is the sound of supernovas exploding in space. It is the sound of the robin singing. It is the sound of a waterfall on a crystal-clear day. It is the sound of the entire manifest universe - and you are that sound."[31]

Ken Wilber

"Muhammed said, 'Make no distinction
between my ascending and Jonah's descending
into the fish. Nearness to God
is beyond ranking and description'
No up, down, soon, far, or late.
Those terms are appropriate only for existence and time."

Rumi

"In this universe the things which appear <u>opposite to each other</u> are nothing but the coming face to face of the variable qualities of God." *Resuhi Baykara*

Part Twenty Seven

THE PARADOX OF PRACTICE

We saw in the chapter on practice in Part Three of this framework how the very idea of practice can appear paradoxical since it is an effort to become what we already are and always have been. Yet many of us derive great benefit from practices such as meditation, turning or yoga etc. We saw how the idea of practice is not so much a concept of trying to reach a different state at some future time, but more an expression of the Universal at this moment. So we practice because we love it and are drawn to it, not because it is something we feel we should do to achieve a particular goal in the future.

The question is often asked, "If we already are the Universal then why the need for practice?" In one answer to this question the Shankaracharya pointed out that it is often by some form of practice that we do become aware that we already are the Universal. If not, our identity can just remain at the superficial level of the drama of life.

A much revered Indian saint from the first half of the 20th century, Ramana Maharshi, taught that in relation to practice there are three types of devotee: those who are like gunpowder, charcoal or wet coal. The gunpowder type of person only needs to have the concept of non-duality explained and realisation is instantaneous, only a single spark is required.

Those that are like charcoal require a little more heat to ignite the charcoal and for these people Ramana Maharshi normally prescribed the practice of Self Enquiry, enquiring into the nature of the Self, following the sense of personal identity back to its source until its Universal nature is perceived at first hand.

The third type, wet coal, usually require some form of systematic practice to gradually dry the coal out to the point of ignition.

The Shankaracharya also indicates the same thing. Some people only need to hear a small part of the teaching and will then work out the whole thing for themselves. With others it takes a little more time. It is this time process in Self Realisation that gives rise to the drama of creation. If we were all born into an instant realisation of our essential unity then the unfolding drama of creation and the apparent process of a gradual return to the Source would be impossible.

So each of us, in our lives, is gradually led on a path to rediscover our essential Oneness. For some people this path will involve being drawn to practice such methods as meditation, turning or yoga. By these systematic methods we gradually become aware of our true identity. We realise that there is a still part of ourselves that is beyond the ups and downs of our individual life dramas, that is always available as a wordless presence. As this process deepens we see that our life dramas and all that surrounds us is also part of this Self and that nothing is separate or outside it.

For many people their particular life path does not include such practices; it is just the living of life that brings about the realisation of the Unity of all things. From our observation of life and the many coincidences that happen in the unfolding of our particular path we may start to get a feeling that we, as separate entities, are not the creators of this drama, that it is all part of a much larger unfolding of which we are all part. For some people it can be a difficult illness or life situation that is the catalyst that causes Consciousness to give up its identity with form.

The words we use for this process of realising our true identity, whether it is instantaneous like 'gunpowder' or covers a greater duration of time like 'wet coal' may differ. We may use such terms as 'practice', 'preparation', 'purification' or 'polishing the mirror' but these are all metaphors for the fact that we may need a little time to turn our attitudes around, to discover the true nature of Reality, that which we already are and always have been.

So it is not a question of we as separate entities seeking to find our way back to the Universal, since the separate entity never existed in the first place. It more a case of Consciousness seeking itSelf as is illustrated in the story of the donkeys who were unable to move because they thought they were bound whereas in reality they were already free.

Quotations

The following four quotations are all from the Shankaracharya:

"In this work on Spirit, there can never be a time-limit for full Realisation. It depends on the state of the Antahkarana of the individual. If it is ready-made at a high level then realisation is very quick, otherwise unless the cleansing process is complete, the realisation would not come about. It may very well take ten or 20 years for some people."

"The Truth is that one really is Atman and the Absolute, but one doesn't know this secret because of ignorance.

There was a dhobi (washerman). He used many donkeys to carry his load. One day he fell ill and asked his son to load the donkeys and take them with the washing. The son loaded them and tried to move them towards the river but they wouldn't budge an inch. Seeing they weren't tied up, he was surprised and went to ask his father. The father said, 'Oh, I should have told you about this! In the evening I touch their feet as if I am trying to bind them with a rope, and in the morning touch them again as if I have undone them.' The boy did the same, and then each donkey started to move. The donkeys felt they were not free; therefore they couldn't walk!

This is the condition of all human beings. The ignorance is illusion."

"For people who regularly come and attend your meetings and try to hear the good words which have already been given and yet do not find the point of rest, the main reason for that is because of their inborn tendencies (Samskar). They have still got in them a certain disturbed element, and due to that they are not able to make their own all that is told to them, and when they go back they again get engulfed in their previous Samskar. They should continue to meditate and reflect again and again about what they have heard so that in due course of time their previous associations will get wiped off and there will be room for taking in the new

things which they have been told.

Similarly, the previous associations are so deep in these people that the element of disturbance is there. That has to be washed off and the only way to do that is by constantly bringing to mind the messages they have heard and thereby they will be able to imbibe them."

"There was a Mahatma living in a secluded place under a tamarind tree. He did his devotional act of meditation every day. There is a deity known as Narada and he is supposed to be the messenger of the Absolute who keeps on descending to earth gathering information to keep the Absolute fully informed. He happened to be making his rounds, and he came upon this Mahatma and engaged him in conversation, wanting to know what he was doing.

The Mahatma said, 'Well, this is all a drama, and at the moment I am engaged in the drama of meditation, and who are you? Narada replied that he was the messenger of the Absolute and came to collect information about all the devotees of God so that he could tell Him about their well-being. The Mahatma said this was excellent, as he could take a message, and Narada said, 'Yes, why not?' The Mahatma said, 'Ask Him when there will be a meeting'.

Narada went away, and came back after some time to the Mahatma, who asked him if there was any reply. Narada said there was a reply, but it was rather a bitter one and he would rather not give it as the Mahatma's heart would sink. The Mahatma said, 'But if there is any reply from the Absolute, my heart would never sink. Don't worry about it, just let me know the answer'.

Narada said, 'Look at this tamarind tree. It has very small leaves and millions of them; as many leaves as there are on this tree you will have to wait the same number of years, after which God will come to meet you; this is the message.'

At this the Mahatma burst into ecstasy, and started dancing with bliss, completely forgetting himself. Narada was quite baffled by this man, who although told he had to wait millions of years before the union could take place, was dancing with joy. He asked, 'Wait - have you really understood what I have said?' The Mahatma replied. 'Yes, I heard,' and Narada said, 'What did you hear?' and the Mahatma said, 'As many leaves as there are on the tamarind tree, so many years will I have to wait and then He will come.' Narada asked 'Then why are you dancing?' The Mahatma said, 'I am not going to count the number of years and the leaves. All that matters is that I have had a message from the Absolute, and He is going to meet me; He will never let me down. That is what really matters'. And once again he started dancing.

At that moment the Absolute Himself descended and embraced the Mahatma. Narada was very disturbed. He said, 'My Lord, I am your messenger, but don't let me be proved a liar. You said it would be so many years, and that is what I told the Mahatma, and you have broken your word and descended immediately! You didn't even wait an hour and you've fulfilled the promise which was supposed to wait years.'

Then the Absolute said, 'These things are for ordinary men; if there is somebody special, then questions of time and space and Gunas have to be ignored and the meeting must be instantaneous'.

The same applies to all these details about people of devotion or people of knowledge. If there is a rare case where there is nothing else, only devotion, nothing but a longing for truth, then the union could take place without delay."

"Doshin, the fourth Chinese Zen patriarch, came to the third patriarch Sosan, and asked to be liberated. Sosan responded, 'Who put you under restraint?' Doshin replied, 'No one.' Sosan asked, 'Then why are you seeking to be liberated?' At that, Doshin had great Satori. As the story illustrates, there are no bonds to be freed from, nothing is lacking, and there is nothing that has to be gained by training. As was said in the very first sentence of this text, 'The Great Way is limitless, fathomless and subtle.'"[32] *Zen Story*

Part Twenty Eight

HAPPINESS

One of the main motivating factors in human life is the pursuit of happiness. However, the way we try to find happiness differs greatly from individual to individual. Some may look for it in possessions, or in relationships, or in status, or longer weekends and holidays or in a variety of other ways.

Anything that exists on the line of time is subject to a beginning and an end. The possession we thought would bring us happiness no longer does so after a while and we find ourselves wanting something more. Relationships, like our jobs, are subject to change or redundancy or a parting of some sort. Weekends and holidays all eventually come to an end.

The psychiatrist and Auschwitz survivor, Viktor Frankl, suggests that if we pursue happiness as an end in itself, it tends to elude us. But it may happen that happiness ensues as a result of devoting ourselves to a cause greater than ourselves. In this way it unexpectedly finds us.

There is, however, another form of happiness that is not dependent on external circumstances. This is the happiness that emerges from within as a result of having a still mind and is an intimation of our true Selves. It can well up from within at unexpected times often when we least expect it and sometimes in the most adverse conditions. An event or situation can unexpectedly bring us into the light of the present which is the only place where this type of deep inner happiness is available.

It is sometimes said in the Advaita tradition that Joy is food for the Atman (Self). This can appear to be a paradoxical statement since happiness is one of the properties of the Self and one of the touchstones by which we recognise it. We can understand this further if we realise that the Self is not somewhere else waiting to be discovered but is our deepest identity. It is through the senses that it looks out and appreciates its own creation. When we are passionate and take delight in the different aspects of life, it is

Consciousness appreciating its own manifestation. This reinforces the importance of having the courage to 'follow our bliss'. This means following that deep inner sense of happiness and rightness wherever it leads us and allowing our motivating factor to be delight rather than duty or guilt.

When we have an abundance of the sattvic energy of Being we can feel a deep happiness or contentment. This is not because sattva itself creates happiness, but because it causes our psyches to become still and transparent like a clear glass. Then the light of the Self is able to flow through us and outwards into all creation so that it is not a question of 'our' happiness but rather that we are just a transparent vehicle for a Universal 'greater happiness'.

The artist Cecil Collins suggested that there is a 'lesser happiness' that exists when events in our lives go our way but there also exists what he called a 'greater happiness' that is independent of circumstances. Perhaps the best way of becoming aware of the 'greater happiness' is when we have total acceptance of 'what is', then we are no longer in opposition to the process of life and its unfolding.

When we desire things in life, whether it is objects, situations or people, the very act of desire takes us out of the present moment awareness and the satisfaction with this moment now as it is. With the fulfilment of our objective, the desire ceases and we return to a feeling of contentment with the present moment. This leads us to believe that happiness came from the object we desired when in reality it was due to a temporary return to a state of no desire. The cause of the happiness was in us and not in the object. As we have seen, after a little while we want something else and the cycle starts again. The remedy for this situation is the realisation that whatever is before us is the manifestation of Consciousness. Whatever is before us is 'It' in all its fullness.

As this attitude gradually permeates our being, so too does a deep inner happiness that is not dependent on passing time but is the nature of who we really are.

Quotations

> *"We feel pleasure in various things, because we take a particle of that Anand which is our nature and throw it into that*

particular thing. Otherwise that thing itself is not an object which will give any pleasure or displeasure. It's because we transfer some of that Anand which is our basic nature of the Param-Atman - that we feel pleasure or displeasure."

The Shankaracharya

"Happiness is the very nature of the Self; happiness and the Self are not different. There is no happiness in any object of the world. We imagine through out ignorance that we derive happiness from objects. When the mind goes out, it experiences misery. In truth, when its desires are fulfilled, it returns to its own place and enjoys the happiness that is the Self. Similarly, in the states of sleep, samaadhi, and fainting, and when the object desires is obtained or the object disliked is removed, the mind becomes inward-turned, and enjoys pure Self-Happiness."[33] *Ramana Maharshi*

"The best way to control desires is to have contentment - the feeling that God alone is the best judge of what is best for me, what He has given me is best for me. And if you have that sort of contentment, then you will be able to control that keen desire and you will feel happy in whatever circumstances you are placed.

A person who can bear with adversities will always remain happy. It's a sort of meal for Atman to remain happy always because we are part and parcel of Sat-Chit-Ananda. Ananda is the quality of God and we are part and parcel of God, therefore we like to be happy and if we are happy, then that is a sort of food for Atman." *The Shankaracharya*

"Either you can accept it as blissful or miserable, it depends on how you place yourself in relation to this drama. If you are attached to the drama, if you think it is real, then the general picture is of misery. If you are detached, if you think it is a drama, and there is a part to be played by you, then it is all blissful." *The Shankaracharya*

"The way to find out about your happiness is to keep your mind on those moments when you feel most happy, when you

really are happy - not excited, not just thrilled, but deeply happy. This requires a little bit of self-analysis. What is it that makes you happy? Stay with it, no matter what people tell you. This is what I call 'following your bliss'."

Joseph Campbell

"The lowest level one could call the small happiness, and above that ... a small unhappiness where one is restricted to fear of losing the small happiness. Above is the great happiness, which means you have seen through the small happiness. I mean by that it doesn't satisfy you, and you are unhappy in a very deep way because you know there's a great happiness, and, if you cannot experience that, you reject every other kind of happiness, because that is the happiness you know to be the greatest and the most real ... Let me put it another way: you are unhappy because you can't reach it but you are very happy because you can see it. In a word, you're alive." *Cecil Collins*

"Don't aim at success - the more you aim at it and make it a target, the more you are going to miss it. For success, like happiness, cannot be pursued; it must ensue, and it only does so as the unintended side-effect of one's personal dedication to a cause greater than oneself or as the by-product of one's surrender to a person other than oneself. Happiness must happen, and the same holds for success, you have to let it happen by not caring about it. I want you to listen to what your conscience commands you do and go on to carry it out to the best of your knowledge. Then you will live to see that in the long run - in the long run, I say! - success follows you precisely because you had forgotten to think of it." *Viktor Frankl*

"Friends you don't arouse people by duty - you can make them feel guilty, maybe you can tire them.

Let it go - friends the idea of duty and morality goes back to Kant and the Enlightenment.

Friends Aquinas said you change people by delight, you change people by pleasure." *Matthew Fox*

"The present moment is always lit." *The Shankaracharya*

"My fiftieth year had come and gone.
I sat, a solitary man,
In a crowded London shop,
An open book and empty cup
On the marble table-top.
While on the shop and street I gazed
My body of a sudden blazed:
And twenty minutes more or less
It seemed so great my happiness,
That I was blessed and could bless."[36]

W.B. Yeats

Part Twenty Nine

GIVING UP

It is an immense relief to discover that in order to realise our full potential nothing needs to be added on. In fact the reverse is true. It is simply a process of letting go of all the things that we are not. What could be simpler than giving up that which we never were in the first place? It all seems to be a bit of a paradox; for the sake of the drama of creation we grow up and learn certain things about ourselves and the world we live in but later we have to let go of them all.

So what exactly is the nature of this giving up? The first notion that needs to be let go of is surely the concept of our identity. We tend to identify our sense of self only with the physical body and our psyche, the mind-body mechanism as it is sometimes called. But throughout this framework we have seen that this is simply not the whole truth. As we progress through life both our bodies and minds are subject to a series of changes. My five year old self is very different from my fifty year old self. So what is permanent and what can I really call 'I'?

We have seen that behind this ever changing identity is our basic sense of 'I AM'. At first this appears to be just our own deep inner identity that is ever present and beyond the changes of the mind and body. But there is also a second stage to this 'I AM' realisation. We discover that this is not just our own deepest identity but is the same 'I AM' of every person and every living creature. Even more, it is the 'I AM' of mountains and oceans, planets and suns, spiral nebulae and the universe of 200 billion galaxies, all of which exist and unfold within this 'Amness'.

This concept of mistaken identity naturally leads on to giving up the very idea of multiplicity. The 8th century Indian teacher Padmasambhava who introduced Buddhism to Tibet (where he is known as Guru Rinpoche) said: "To see things as a multiplicity and so cleave unto separateness is to err." This is a very key statement and contains the essence of Advaita. As we come to realise our own true identity the world of multiplicity vanishes as does the concept of 'others' and with that the idea of 'blame'. The world and everything in it starts to appear as the display of the One Mind, a dynamic dance where everything is seen as inseparable aspects of one undivided whole.

The giving up of the sense of multiplicity leads naturally to the giving up of the sense of personal doing. We can look back over our lives and it can appear like a well-written drama or film. Characters often appear in our lives, play necessary roles and then disappear and we do the same for others, not as separate entities but as parts of one whole. With this outlook there arises a giving up of the need to manipulate life and other people. We begin to develop a deep trust in life's unfolding where we take the necessary action in accordance with the needs of the moment. Then we are always in the right place which is such a relief as it allows life to be lived with confidence and patience in the knowledge of who it really is that lives.

The giving up of the sense of being a separate doer of one's actions also leads to a giving up of the sense of ownership. As the very notion of a separate self is seen to be illusory, so too is the notion of ownership, for who is there to own what? We own nothing. Everything we appear to own is simply on loan as part of the drama. Yet, at the same time, from the fullest point of view we own everything.

This can be seen in a very practical way when we look about us. Does anybody own the morning mist in the valley? Who owns the waves on the sea or the clouds in the sky? Which corporation owns the Milky Way that I see stretching across the sky on still clear nights. Do I have to pay a royalty for lying on my back looking up at it? No, it's all there to be enjoyed and then to be let go of.

There is a further aspect to the concept of giving up and that is the giving up of suffering. Unlike physical pain, suffering is often psychological and usually relates to the past or the future. The things we fear or are anxious about usually belong to the future. The things we have regret or sorrow about are usually in the past. We can test the validity of this claim by asking ourselves what is actually wrong at this moment now as we read this or hear this - not tomorrow or in five minutes or half an hour ago - but now!

So it is the separate self that suffers and the separate self exists only in the past or future. As we let go of the constant mental chatter through which we interpret life, all that exists is this moment and then the next. In this moment now there only exists the Universal and this moment now is all that ever exists.

Quotations

"One of the essential illusions that you have to give up is that you are a separate person from the rest of creation, and therefore a doer of your actions; whereas your actions and all other actions are a part of an extremely complicated pattern that you cannot alter." *Dr Roles*

"Whatever one sees in creation, all that lives and moves - one should use it fully and enjoy the Absolute in everything, but one should enjoy it with renunciation. One should not try to hold it or covet it. Just because the Absolute is always everywhere, one need not try to hold it; enjoy it - and give it up. 'Giving up' is the most simple philosophy which promises complete fulfilment of the individual's life, also liberation after having enjoyed it." *The Shankaracharya*

"Attachment means to consider as ours what really belongs to God. Our body, our house, our wealth, our son etc. Give up this feeling and you get rid of all your troubles. Do not think that the world around you is insubstantial. Rather it is your feeling of attachment to it that is insubstantial. Whatever is happening around you is right. What is wrong about it is the view you are taking of it. If you could correct your viewpoint, you would be happy."

The Shankaracharya

"Giving up can be done mentally and intellectually at all times and in all conditions. In this, there is no question of today or tomorrow, or of one or two days a week. Practise giving up all the time. You just consider the body, the mind and the intellect as belonging to the Param-Atman, and as offering all these to Param-Atman. This is what giving up means." *The Shankaracharya*

The thief forgot
to steal it
The moon at
the window

Haiku

"How should a rock be covered with verdure by the Spring? Become earth, that thou mayst grow flowers of many a hue.

Years hast thou been a heart-jagging rock: once, for the sake of experiment, be earth!"[3] *Rumi*

"When you have given up <u>everything</u> you ordinarily call "I", then your spirit (the Atman) rises, and you have this feeling of expansion, because your spirit is no longer weighted down by all the characteristics associated with "I". So, if you could give up all that, then this expansion would be felt." *Dr Roles*

"Cultivate "I have nothing of my own"; then "The whole universe belongs to me." *Dr Roles*

Part Thirty

REALISATION

In the non-dual traditions of the world we are continually reassured that we are liberated already. All that is lacking is that we tend not to realise this and as a result perceive ourselves as limited and bound rather than limitless and free.

Part of the problem may be a lack of satisfaction with our lives as they are. It is easy to have a projected picture of how we should be, based perhaps on a combination of the Dalai Lama, the Buddha, Mother Theresa and Nelson Mandela all rolled into one. Or there may be any number of possible variations on that theme. But, within the drama, we all play different roles that are each an integral part of the whole so that who we are at any moment is exactly who we are meant to be. This means that a large part of realisation is concerned with simply being ourselves and realising that how we are is just fine. We are not required to get to another place or be someone else. We do not have to travel to any place to have this realisation. If we do not find it here then we will not find it there.

In our lives we are each led along our own tailor-made path to the realisation of our true identity and the true nature of reality. We may find that we have particular talents to develop and are drawn to particular types of activity. Sometimes we are led along a varied path learning different skills whose purpose, at the time, we cannot see. There may be periods of outward success when our lives seem to be building up and other times when everything seems to fall away. Yet it is these events of life that can take us back in the causal chain of identity into the greater depths of ourselves.

At a certain stage our motivation may be more toward the outward aspects of life such as career, position, possessions etc. We may try to seek security at this level of the drama. As we progress through life we find that many of these goals are transitory and limited and that, due to the impermanent nature of life at this level, security cannot be found. So, by the very process of living, we are led to turn inwards to find our security in the only place it can be found - our own true identity that is ever present, quietly observing the changing drama.

Our route to realisation may or may not include certain practices such as meditation or yoga, though we will each be led to the approach that is most suited to our natures and this may vary at different times in our lives.

As we go through all these experiences there gradually arises a sense of being transparent. At first it just comes in flashes but then gradually this feeling starts to permeate all of our being as if the separate entity no longer exists and we are just a window for something that is awesome, all knowing, full of love and is our true Self and the Universal all at once. A deep background stillness, like a fathomless well, begins to pervade our being. The psychology with which we had previously identified now appears as just a surface display.

Some people have this quality not long before they die. It is as if the separate self has already dissolved and the true Being is shining out as a quality of warmth, humour and light. Others develop this quality much earlier in life.

In many of the world's religious and mystical traditions full realisation is often due to the interaction of a teacher, as can be seen in many of the Zen stories. Although it is the same Consciousness manifesting as a teacher and also manifesting through all the other varied aspects of creation that we meet during our life's journey, none of which are accidental, the final catalyst may be through the intervention of a teacher. It might also come through hearing or reading a particular phrase or seeing a leaf fall in autumn or even having an illness or some other difficult life event.

In some traditions the death of the physical body is seen as a moment of great opportunity when everything that has defined our sense of self falls away and we are left with pure Being. Then those aspects of life that had appeared as accidental or pointless are seen now as part of the preparation for this great moment of letting go. Just as we can learn to trust the process of life's unfolding, so too can we trust this ultimate moment of letting go into our true Being.

Quotations

"All individuals are the Absolute themselves, and so are you. It is only a question of realising that one is the Absolute. To realise that, one has to do away with those impediments, and to illustrate this here is a story about a lion cub.

Once, in the forest, a lioness who had several cubs went off to search for food and while she was away, one of the cubs strayed into the middle of a flock of sheep. The cub followed the sheep and the shepherd, seeing the cub with the sheep, kept him. The cub behaved like the sheep because of the company of the sheep. The shepherd thought that, if he remained in this forest, then one day the lioness would roar and the cub, hearing the roar, would remember it was a lion and would attack the sheep. So he took the flock with the cub to another forest where he believed there were no lions.

One day a lion did roar in this other forest and all the sheep ran away, and the cub also tried to run away. The lion - in lion language! - told the cub to stop and said, 'Why are you afraid of me? There is no need; you are not a sheep. You are a lion like me. If you are not sure I can show you.' So he took him to a pond and the little lion saw in the reflection that he had the same face and same characteristics as the one who roared. Then the lion asked him to roar with him, so he learnt how to roar, and the whole personality and individuality of this little lion was completely changed and he started roaring like a grown lion."

The Shankaracharya

"Everyone is free but thinks that they are bound. In fact all those things that bind them are the expression of their own ignorance. This is what everyone has to understand. Here is an example. A special trick is used to catch monkeys. A round earthen pot with a small mouth is buried in the ground. Pieces of tasty food are put inside. When the monkeys smell them, they come close and put their hands inside and clutch the food, and then they cannot pull them out. The monkey doesn't know that he can be free. He doesn't want

to release the piece of food, and yet wants to be free, so he cries, and can't run away. At that moment the man appears from his hiding place and catches the monkey. Most people who think that they are not free are acting like the monkey. They are holding on to something, maybe things of beauty or fragrance. If only they could release their hold, they would be free, because in truth they are free."

The Shankaracharya

"The Supreme Brahman is, like the sky, pure, absolute, infinite, motionless and changeless, devoid of interior or exterior, the One Existence, without a second, and is one's own Self. Is there any other object of knowledge (than Brahman)?"[37] *Shankara*

"What is most difficult of all? It is not to desire the whole world and my own situation to change, but to bring about this change without desiring it, by sincerely and from the depths of my heart entrusting to the hands of God the fate of those dearest to me, my fate and the fate of the whole world; for these are God's own fate."[38] *Petru Demitriu*

"When you are delivered from this place and go to that place, you will give thanks to God in the sugar-shop of everlastingness.

You will say, 'There in the world below I was sifting dust, I was fleeing from this pure world.'

Alas, would that I had died ere now, so that my time of being tormented in the mud might have been less!"[3]

Rumi

"The arising and the elimination of illusion are both illusory. Illusion is not something rooted in Reality; it exists because of your dualistic thinking. If you will only cease to indulge in opposed concepts such as 'ordinary' and 'Enlightened', illusion will cease of itself."[20] *Huang Po*

"For a long time it had seemed to me that life was about to begin - real life. But there was always some obstacle in the

way, something to be got through first, some unfinished business, time still to be served, a debt to be paid. Then life would begin. At last it dawned on me that these obstacles were my life." *Fr. Alfred D'Souza*

"Your true nature is something never lost to you even in moments of delusion, nor is it gained at the moment of Enlightenment."[20] *Huang Po*

"Man is not a creator, he is a reflector, witness, an image and likeness of that which is - the only activity there is - the infinite Mind unfolding itself to itself perpetually in the most glorious, harmonious set of completely specified and detailed forms." *Glen Schaefer*

"At this, Emmon sighed deeply. That sound filled the ten directions. Suddenly the sound stopped and he had great Satori. The mysterious light of clear wisdom radiated of itself and dispelled all doubt. Only now he knew how hard it is to follow the Way, and that as in a dream he had till now been agitated to no purpose. He exclaimed, 'But how marvellous and splendid! Just as the Master has taught without teaching, so I have truly heard without hearing. When hearing and teaching become one, all is wide and vast, oneness without words."[39]

"Emmon, on becoming enlightened, had also awareness of his delusions. These, without his troubling himself in any way about them, had now vanished of themselves. Delusions and faults do not have to be eradicated. They cease to be the moment they are realised. And enlightenment is not gaining something which from that moment onwards becomes one's possession, but is rather the shedding of all delusions, errors, and notions. As that, it is the voiding of everything that obscures truth and prevents it from revealing itself."[32]

"Thusness means everything just as it is, the nature of truth, 'just so'. Grass, trees, men, all manifested forms reveal the truth or are the appearance of truth (in form). But men do not perceive truth as such, just as it is, and now

rather seek it elsewhere. Therefore, to become aware again that everything, just as it is, in its suchness, is the truth called the attainment of Buddhahood."[32]

Extracts from "The Ceasing of Notions" A Zen text from the Tun-Huang caves circa 7th century.

Part Thirty One

THE PATHLESS PATH

There is a recurring theme in the non-dual traditions, that of going on a journey to find a great treasure. In the end we discover the treasure was never absent but was in our own house all the time. In the Sufi tradition Rumi refers to this as the "the Pathless path". In Zen it is sometimes called the "Gateless Gate". Dr Roles, to indicate how simple it all is, told the story of three men who spent a life time trying to climb a wall and when they got to the top all burst out laughing because they had discovered that, in reality, there is no wall at all.

In this chapter we will examine the nature of this path and the nature of the treasure and the fact that it is simple, ever present and freely available, as Dr Roles indicated.

There are often a series of stages in this journey. When we are very young we feel a natural sense of unity with all around us. As we grow up we start to develop a separate sense of self and a separate ego, necessary for relating to others and to the outside world. We then become aware of the many possibilities that life has to offer as we work to develop our careers and build up our material lives and whatever it is we want at the level of life's drama. Very often, when we have achieved many of our goals, we are still left with a feeling of lack, as if whatever we have achieved has never quite satisfied us so that we are always wanting more. Sometimes it is a feeling that the happiness and satisfaction we have been seeking is still eluding us. It can be like a vague memory of something we really want, or have lost but can't quite find again. We have looked for it in achievements and possessions but still it eludes us.

Often at this stage there comes some sort of crisis in life and we become disillusioned with trying to find contentment at this level. This can be precipitated by a difficult life situation such as an illness, relationship break up or loss of financial security. The process may start very early in life with the death of a parent or school friend. There then arises the feeling that there is more to life than just the surface display. It is not that life is rejected, but it ceases to be seen as an end in itself.

This stage can be a turning point and at this time often a search begins. It is a search for a meaning beyond what day to day life has to offer. We may start to look inwards to find our happiness and security in a direction that is a little more permanent. We may be attracted to systematic methods such as meditation. As our practice matures we start to find that there exists an inner source of contentment that is beyond the ups and downs of daily life. At this stage in our path, experiences can be very important. We may want more of these moments of intense happiness but however much we practise, these experiences always seem to be of finite duration in time and space. We may be left seeing consciousness as something that lies in the future when our search finally comes to an end and we have reached a permanent exalted state. At this point in our search there is both a stumbling block and a great opportunity.

The stumbling block is that in pursuing a special state of Consciousness which exists at some time in the future it is always going to elude us and we will only have a glimmer here and a glimmer there so that, like our search for happiness in material gain, it will still not fully satisfy.

When we search for Consciousness we are very like Rumi's story of the fish who swam off to find the stuff called water. By seeking Consciousness in a special future state achievable only once we have done all the necessary work, we will always miss the fact that it is only ever here right now. In this sense seeking and wanting something that we feel we don't already have can ultimately become a means of avoidance.

The opportunity which comes at this stage of the path or journey, when we have searched both the outer world and the idea of special future states of Consciousness, is that we begin to realize and notice that there is nothing to look for.

We've missed what we are looking for because it's so close. So close that it's overlooked as too obvious and simple. It's rather like trying to look at your eyes without the aid of a mirror; it's impossible since they are the instrument of seeing so how can they see themselves? It's just the same with Consciousness. It has only eluded us as an object to find since it is itself the subject; it is already looking out through our eyes, hearing through our ears and sensing through all our other senses, right now. It was just as present before our search began; we haven't uncovered it or developed it one iota. All that has happened is that the search has been exhausted and a recognition has taken place. As Rumi observed, what we are searching for is "closer than our own jugular vein."

We have lived with a consensus view of our identity as a result of identifying with the vehicle of Consciousness and not with the Consciousness itself. When we relax into what is looking out through our eyes, at first there is just nothing. It is like a vast still empty spaciousness that is also an immense fullness from which our thoughts feelings and desires are arising and returning. Happiness arises and returns, fear arises and returns. Our entire lives arise and return. All activity is just a ripple on the surface of this vastness. We are all just the waves on a great ocean of stillness. It is formless and has no boundary. It is totally ordinary and ever present. Every aspect of our lives without exception, the triumphs as well as the broken dreams, are all a part of the pathless path, the journey to acknowledge that which was never lost and can never be found, was never more nor less.

There occurs at this point a total letting go of conceptual frameworks, a ceasing of notions and an opening up into the simplicity of what is. This is very succinctly expressed in the Advaita tradition by the words "Sat Chit Ananda". As we have seen Sat means 'I AM'. It is pure Being, the still spaciousness that is our true identity. Chit is the simple acknowledgement of that pure Being; there exists no other to affect that acknowledgement than the pure Being itself, so it is pure Self awareness. Ananda is the deep, still, unchanging happiness that arises from this acknowledgement and is the nature of that pure Being.

So the pathless path is not a journey to attain or reach anything, but a process of being led to the simple acknowledgement of what "is". As is taught in the Zen tradition, no one actually becomes a Buddha, you simply cease to be deluded.

Quotations

"There's never been a single thing;
Then where's defiling dust to cling?" *Hui Neng*

"The Absolute is Truth, Consciousness and Bliss. The creation is for bliss. It is a play, and the play is only for enjoyment. Human begins are also the Absolute and include everything the Absolute has. Men are self-truthful, self-consciousful and self-blissful. The Absolute creates and enjoys without getting involved, only as a witness, but man prefers to enjoy as a doer and not as a witness. This claim is followed by the duality of 'want it' and 'got it'. All this binds man in little boundaries and little boundaries give him only little bliss. The Self, being the Absolute, could not be satisfied with such little bliss, and this is why there is constant search for more bliss, more truth and more consciousness. The search makes men overactive and run amok which is followed by troubles, anxieties, conflicts and discomfort. The real purpose is thus completely lost. Only if men could see that they have nothing to do, nothing to claim, nothing to achieve in this already complete and blissful creation, they would begin to enjoy and also fulfil the purpose.

The Shankaracharya

"The best you can do is get good at being you."

Dennis the Menace

"For some, given the degree of pain and stress, unhappiness and confusion, etc. it is important to, out of kindness, provide people with a sense of direction, of practice, of going from A to B and getting them well established on the path. It's a perfectly useful resource to do so.

Woe be to those who dismiss it all at hand and say, "Practice is just striving; it's just ego; it's just desire. To take support away from people in that way shows a lack of wisdom and a lack of kindness and a clinging to a view that there's nothing you can do. That view does have to be watched carefully. It's unfair to people who come with great need and great longing for well-being, happiness, and peace in their life, to then be told that there is nothing they can do. It leaves some people disheartened and despairing.

There are others, of course, who respond to "nothing to do" by questioning any holding and clinging to their form of structure, and become free of it. But I have listened to many voices of those who have been hurt by major charismatic authority figures saying there is nothing you can do. And, one can also be hurt by those who say that it is a long, long, long, hard road."[41] *Christopher Titmuss*

"Know that form springs from spirit (reality as the lion from the jungle, or as voice and speech from thought).
This speech and voice arose from thought; thou knowest not where is the sea of thought,
But since thou hast seen that the waves of speech are fair, thou knowest that their sea also is noble.

When the waves of thought sped on from (the sea of) Wisdom, it (Wisdom) made (for them) the form of speech and voice.
The form was born of the Word and died again, the wave drew itself back into the sea.
The form came forth from Formlessness and went back (thither), for Verily unto Him are we returning."[3]

Rumi

"I'd like to tell you a story which shows that everything is so simple, really, compared with the complexity that we make of it: Three men spent a lifetime trying laboriously to climb a wall, and when at last they succeeded, the first man laughed so much that he never came back. He jumped down and disappeared for keeps. The second man laughed inordinately. He laughed so hard that he fell down on the wrong side of the wall, and suffered multiple injuries. But the third man laughed in a good-natured kind of way, and came back to help his friends. But there is no wall. that's what everyone was laughing at. There's no wall at all!" *Dr Roles*

"Learn the secret of happiness from the Prophet, and be happy with whatever God gives you.

If you are patient and content with whatever comes onto you and do not complain, instantly the doors of heaven open to you. If the messenger of sorrows comes to you, receive him as an old friend and hug him. he is not a stranger to you; you surely have acquaintance with him.

Do not show a sour face toward the adversity that comes from the Beloved, receive it with joy. Say "Hello and welcome!" Show a smiling face and say nice words so that that unique, beautiful being removes its unpleasant cover and shows its beauty. Firmly grasp at the end of the cover of that beautiful being that came covered with sorrow. Never release it. Do not think about the dirtiness of the cover. The being under the cover is very beautiful, sweet, and faithful."

Rumi

"All you need is to give up your learning', your 'ignorant' and 'Enlightened', 'pure' and 'impure', 'great' and 'little', your 'attachment' and 'activity'. Such things are mere conveniences, mere ornaments with the One Mind.

So just discard all you have acquired as being no better than a bed spread for you when you were sick. Only when you have abandoned all perception, there being nothing objective to perceive; only when phenomena obstruct you no longer; only when you have rid yourself of the whole gamut of dualistic concepts of the 'ignorant' and 'Enlightened' category, will you at last earn the title of Transcendental Buddha."[20] *Huang Po*

"Jesus said: 'Become passers by'".[4] *Gospel of Thomas*

"The pathless path opens whenever you genuinely say, 'There is no reality but God. There is only God.'" *Rumi*

"BEHIND THE VEIL

Neither you nor I
know the secrets of pre-eternity.

Neither you nor I
have grasped the deepest mystery.

Now we are speaking
beside the veil -

But once that curtain is lifted,
neither you
nor I
will remain."[42]

Abu 'l-Hasan Kharaqani

REFERENCES

1 Joseph Campbell, "The Power of Myth", Doubleday
2 P.D. Ouspensky "Tertium Organum" p.227, Routledge and Kegan Paul, 1981
3 Jalaluddin Rum Mathnawi, translated by Dr Reynold A. Nicholson, Luzac & Co. pub. by the trustees of the E.J.W. Gibb Memoral Trust.
4 "The Gospel of Thomas" Nag Hammadi Library, E.J. Brill, Leiden.
5 Ken Wilber, "The Eye of Spirit" used by arrangement with Shambhala Publications inc.
6 Benjamin Hoff, "The Tao of Pooh" Mandarin 1989.
7 Robert Bly, "The Light Around the Body", copyright © 1967 by Robert Bly. Copyright renewed 1995 by Robert Bly, reprinted by permission of HarperCollins Publishers.
8 Herman Hesse, "Siddhartha" copyright © 1951 by New Directions Publishing Corp., reprinted by permission of New Directions Publishing Corp.
9 Ken Wilber, "One Taste" used by arrangement with Shambhala Publications inc.
10 Stephen Levine, "Healing into Life and Death", Anchor Books 1987. reprinted with permission from Random House, Inc.
11 Stephen Levine, "Meetings at the Edge", Gateways Books, 1984.
12 D. Mudaliar, "Day by Day with Bhagavan" p222, Sri Ramanasramam.
13 Ramana Maharshi, "Self Enquiry", Sri Ramanasramam 1971.
14 Julian of Norwich, "Revelations of Divine Love" p.80 Penguin 1966.
15 Thorwald Dethlefsen and Rudiger Dahlke, "The Healing Power of Illness" Element 1990.
16 Gerald Priestland, "The Case against God" p.118, Collins 1984.
17 Lao Tzu, "Tao Te Ching", translated by Stephen Mitchell. HarperCollins 1988.
18 Helen Thomas, "World Without End", Faber and Faber Ltd.
19 Lama Anagarika Govinda, "The Way of the White Clouds, p.84 Rider 1992. Reprinted by permission of The Random House Group Ltd.
20 John Blofield (Editor and Translator), "The Zen Teaching of Huang Po", The Buddhist Society, 1968.
21 T.N. Venkataraman, "Maharshi's Gospel" p.31, Sri Ramanasramam.
22 The Gospel of Thomas, "The Nag Hammadi Library", translated by Thomas O. Lambdin, E.J. Brill, Leiden 1977.
23 Sogyol Rinpoche, "Glimpse after Glimpse", Rider 1995, reprinted by permission of Random House Group Ltd and HarperCollins (US/Canadian Rights)
24 Acts of Thomas "Apocryphal New Testament" p.413 Vs 43-47, translated by M.R. James, Oxford University Press.
25 Quoted in "Handbook for the Soul", edited by Richard Carlson and Benjamin Shield, Piatkus 1996.

26 Eckhart Tolle, "The Power of Now", copyright 1999 by Eckhart Tolle, reprinted with permission of New World Library, CA, www.newworldlibrary.com.
27 Matthew Fox, "Original Blessing", Bear and Co Inc. 1983.
28 Peter and Elizabeth Fenwick, "The Truth in the Light", Hodder Headline.
29 George Ritchie, "Return from Tomorrow" p.48, Kingsway Publications 1978.
30 Brian Sibley, "Shadowlands", Hodder and Stoughton.
31 Ken Wilber, "A Brief History of Everything" p.230, used by arrangement with Shambhala Publications Inc.
32 "The Ceasing of Notions", The Zen Centre London 1988, from the commentary by Soko Morinaga Roshi.
33 Ramana Maharshi, "Who Am I?" p.11, Sri Ramanasramam 12th Edition 1969.
34 William Anderson, "Cecil Collins, The Quest for the Great Happiness" p.12, Barrie and Jenkins Ltd. 1988.
35 Viktor Frankl, "Man's Search for Meaning", Washington Square Press 1984.
36 W.B. Yeats, "The Winding Stair", reprinted with permission from A.P.Watt Ltd on behalf of Michael B. Yeats.
37 Shankara, "Viveka-Chudamani" Swami Madhavananda, Advaita Ashrama 1944.
38 Petru Demitriu, "Incognito", Collins.
39 "The Ceasing of Notions". Some scholars attribute this text to Bodhidharma, the first Zen patriarch. Recent opinion attributes it to Niu-tou Fa-jung (594-657), The Zen Centre, London 1988.
40 P.D. Ouspensky, "A New Model of the Universe" p.325, Routledge and Kegan Paul Ltd. 1938
41 Lynn Marie Lumiere and John Lumiere-Wins, editors, "The Awakening West" p.68, Fair Winds Press 2003.
42 "Love's Alchemy" translated by David and Sabrinch Sideler, New World Library © 2006.